D0349811

Emotion
Marketing

Emotion Marketing

The Hallmark Way of Winning Customers for Life

SCOTT ROBINETTE
AND
CLAIRE BRAND
WITH VICKI LENZ

McGraw-Hill

NEW YORK   SAN FRANCISCO   WASHINGTON, D.C.   AUCKLAND   BOGOTÁ
CARACAS   LISBON   LONDON   MADRID   MEXICO CITY   MILAN
MONTREAL   NEW DELHI   SAN JUAN   SINGAPORE
SYDNEY   TOKYO   TORONTO

McGraw-Hill

A Division of The McGraw·Hill Companies

Copyright © 2001 by Hallmark Cards. All rights reserved. Printed in the United States of America. Except as permitted under the United States Copyright Act of 1976, no part of this publication may be reproduced or distributed in any form or by any means, or stored in a data base or retrieval system, without the prior written permission of the publisher.

The following terms are trademarks or service marks of Hallmark Licensing, Inc.: Hallmark, Hallmark Loyalty Marketing Group, The Value Star, Emotional Marketing, Relationship-Building Scorecard, Binney & Smith, Crayola, The Crayola Factory, Silly Putty, Party Express, Shoebox, Tree of Life, Warm Wishes, Keepsake Ornament, Hallmark Gold Crown, Hallmark Entertainment, Hallmark Hall of Fame, Hallmark Business Expressions. Penmanship Printing is a trademark of Irresistible Ink, Inc.

1 2 3 4 5 6 7 8 9 0   DOC / DOC   0 9 8 7 6 5 4 3 2 1 0

ISBN 0-07-136414-5

This book was set in Granjon by North Market Street Graphics.
Printed and bound by R.R. Donnelley & Sons Company.

McGraw-Hill books are available at special quantity discounts to use as premiums and sales promotions, or for use in corporate training programs. For more information, please write to the Director of Special Sales, Professional Publishing, McGraw-Hill, Two Penn Plaza, New York, NY 10121-2298. Or contact your local bookstore.

This book is printed on recycled, acid-free paper containing a minimum of 50% recycled, de-inked fiber.

The last several years have been a remarkable time for Hallmark Loyalty Marketing Group. We always knew we were onto something big—leveraging emotion to inspire brand loyalty and drawing from Hallmark's experience enhancing personal connections to help our clients strengthen their business relationships.

Now we have the stories, the studies, and the results to back up all our instincts, and we couldn't be happier—or more excited to continue building our momentum.

But first, the authors wish to sincerely thank the following people for supporting us, pushing us further, and being with us during this first stage of what's sure to be a long, fulfilling journey . . .

Our families for their unwavering love and support.

Our colleagues and business partners whose passion, creativity, and commitment to excellence are the fuel for Emotion Marketing.

Our consumers around the world who show they care enough to send the very best every day.

Our business clients whose practical application of, and investment in, Emotion Marketing are creating a new standard for customer loyalty.

And the Hall family, whose vision and leadership are wonderful examples for us and make the legacy of Hallmark what it is today.

And last, for the dozens of people who invested their time, energy, and talents to making this book a reality—with special acknowledgment to Tom Shirkey, Paul Treacy, and Trish Berrong.

We look forward to many more great years ahead.

Contents

Part Three
How to Put Emotion Marketing to Work

Foreword

It has been generally known and accepted for more than a decade that it costs less to retain customers than to acquire them. That a majority of consumers and business customers prefer to buy from people they know and like—and are willing to pay a bit more to do so. That business relationships built and maintained over time translate into long-term business growth and success. And yet we continue to struggle with how to nurture customer relationships, how to deliver better value, how to create greater customer satisfaction, and how to get to know our customers better.

Companies in virtually every business category must deal with the effects of rapid change, new competition, and shifting customer loyalties. Hallmark is no different. And as we continue to evolve and grow our business to anticipate new areas of consumer interest and demand, we believe we have found a *constant* underlying all those dynamics. That constant is *caring about the customer.* Really, truly caring in a genuine, relevant way. This kind of caring can be difficult to deliver, day after day across a diverse range of business relationships.

At Hallmark, relationships have always been at the heart of our business. This is true in both the expressions of thought and emotion, and in our working relationship with thousands of retailers and other businesses around the world. In 1910 when my grandfather started what was to become Hallmark, his inventory of cards could be kept in a shoe box. He grew the business through personal selling relationships and an uncompromising commitment to deliver the highest possible quality to customers. Along the way a corporate culture grew around caring—caring about our employees, caring about our business customers, and caring about the millions of consumers who purchase our products.

Over the years, we have built on our tradition of caring for the consumer and demanding excellence on their behalf in the products and services we deliver. With the creation of Hallmark Loyalty Marketing Group, formerly Hallmark Business Expressions, in 1995, we began sharing with other companies the insights and successful concepts Hallmark has incorporated in our own customer loyalty programs. We have been fortunate to work with many client companies that are striving for the same goal of continually improving employee and customer relationships. Hallmark Loyalty Marketing Group is becoming a primary resource for companies interested in implementing emotion-based communications solutions to enhance their business relationships.

Because of our interest and growing involvement in emotion-based marketing, we welcome the opportunity to share our experience with you. Author Vicki Lenz has been involved in our client symposiums on relationship marketing. As author of *The Saturn Difference* and president of "Emphasis on Customers!" Vicki has already brought insights on caring about the customer to the forefront. Once we recognized our joint interest in emotion marketing, we formalized our insights into some useful "tools" for business decision-making. You'll see how Hallmark and other companies have applied this strategic relationship framework to their organization and marketplace challenges.

Emotion Marketing is central to delivering value and creating customer loyalty—as a means to profit, growth, and long-term business success. What it really means is strong relationships are good for business, and expressions of caring can help you strengthen relationships with employees and customers. I hope you find these insights useful in building your success.

Don Hall, Jr.
Corporate Vice President
of Strategy and Development
Hallmark Cards, Inc.

Preface

If you're like most professionals we've encountered, when first introduced to the concept of Emotion Marketing, you'll find it somewhat perplexing—it conjures up reactions of both skepticism and intrigue. Can a business whose goal is to increase the propensity on the part of the consumer to repurchase truly have an "emotional" relationship with its customers?

Let's start by defining emotion in this context. Trust is the emotion of business. Achieving a high level of trust comes to those businesses that earn it and are motivated by win-win decision-making. It definitely gets results. But maybe you're not so easily convinced. On the one hand, perhaps since you weren't likely taught the subject in business school, you find it difficult to believe that investing hard cash in the intangibles can be justified as a legitimate business strategy. On the other hand, you can't prove that providing emotional benefits doesn't play some sort of role in the success of a given enterprise.

Chances are you were drawn to this book because your intuition tells you there's something real and powerful about how emotion affects our daily lives. Maybe you've experienced for yourself how your heart led you to make a decision against your head's better judgment. That car you paid more for than your budget allowed, that tropical vacation you traded two months' salary to experience, those shoes you just had to have that only go with one outfit, that expensive golf club that promised to fix your slice. Or, if you're a student of consumer behavior, maybe you've observed your customers acting in ways contrary to what you expected, or behaving completely differently than they said they would in focus groups or survey research. Somewhere, deep down, you just *know* the realm of emotion makes a difference. So how does one make sense of this mysterious paradox?

The fact that you're reading this now hints to the answer, and the underlying truth of this book—*human beings (yes, even males) are emotional creatures who have a deep-rooted need to connect with each other and the world around them.* Our emotions serve a critically important role in our quest to survive, thrive, and realize our full potential. Emotion brings depth and meaning to life. It bridges the gap between our innermost needs and our daily actions to achieve satisfaction. It moves us to act, to participate in the game of life. It validates our decisions and empowers us to feel good or bad about them. It helps us navigate through hundreds— if not thousands—of decisions we make every day. Without emotion, life is stripped of its meaning, its essence, its experiential value, its rewards.

If there's one thing we've learned after nearly 90 years of leadership in the relationship business, it's that *emotion matters.* From brand building and employee satisfaction to product leadership and customer loyalty, nearly every major success at Hallmark can be traced to the effective creation, utilization, delivery, or exchange of emotional value. We've come to know firsthand that our success in sustaining competitive advantage in the marketplace is directly correlated with our ability to establish and strengthen an emotional connection between Hallmark and our key stakeholders.

Over the years, as the success of Hallmark gained exposure and recognition in marketing circles, other companies increasingly turned to us for benchmarking, best practices, and advice on building lasting bonds with their customers and employees. In 1995, Hallmark Loyalty Marketing Group—originally named Hallmark Business Expressions—was formed to respond to these numerous requests and provide a center-of-excellence for the profitable pursuit of customer loyalty. Since its inception, the group has emerged as one of Hallmark's fastest growing business units, helping hundreds of the world's most revered and respected organizations add emotional value in their business relationships.

Our adventure began with a rigorous study of the customer loyalty field. We conducted an exhaustive review of what loyalty experts were finding, benchmarked the best practices of other companies with successful loyalty initiatives, and cross-referenced those trends with our own experience in building loyalty within Hallmark. As we began working with other companies, it became abundantly clear that the power of Emotion Marketing was not being leveraged, and that most attempts at building loyalty were falling short of their full potential. We saw the initial advantage of traditional frequency or "points-based" programs begin to fade as more and more competitors jumped into the loyalty game. Above all else, we heard consumers everywhere crying out to be recognized, valued, and appreciated.

We knew we had a story to tell, and our passion to get the message out grew rapidly. It wasn't enough to whisper in the ear of a few companies. As pioneers in the caring business, we felt a responsibility to shout it out to the world—if for no other reason than to restore the waning consumer trust in business institutions. We also knew that most successful marketers had utilized elements of Emotion Marketing in their past mass marketing efforts, positioning their products where they make a difference in people's lives. (And yes, babies and puppies in commercials have always worked!) However, there was a thirst for knowledge as to how to translate that to the more individualized, one-to-one marketing arena that extends beyond product to service and relationships without seeming awkward or contrived. For this reason we decided it was time to write the book on Emotion Marketing.

As Stephen Covey said, "All real progress begins with a paradigm shift—a break with." It is our sincere desire that the insights and examples contained in this book give you a new lens through which you can view the competitive landscape and provide the impetus for real change in your organization. We hope it instructs, informs, and inspires you to harness the power of emotion across your enterprise to deliver what your customers desperately need—the personal attention, respect, and admiration they deserve. As we've learned firsthand, they're ready and willing to give their loyalty—and their business—to those companies who earn the right to *win customers for life.*

Claire Brand
Scott Robinette

Did you ever have an "Ah-ha!" moment? One of those rare times when suddenly everything came together and made perfect sense? And it's so basic, you wonder why you didn't see it before?

Mine came after two and one-half decades in marketing, during a discussion with the people at Hallmark Loyalty Marketing Group (a division of Hallmark Cards Inc.). They described their research, experience, and practical applications of the role that emotion plays in the customer loyalty equation. EMOTION. That's it! Suddenly, I realized that emotion was the one-and-only, really true basis of successful marketing and the secret to value, customer loyalty, and profits.

Think about it. Your decisions to buy are based on emotion. Sure, there's rational thought involved, but one way or another you—and what you value—are influenced by emotion. Many times, emotion holds the rational mind captive. On the other side, businesses strive to create more value for customers and increase loyalty by subscribing to relationship management, loyalty programs, and one-to-one marketing. But what's the common thread—the missing link necessary to achieve the real competitive edge? Emotion! And it's been around from the very beginning. It's just that nobody figured how it fits into the marketing equation, and how it provides value that adds up to customer loyalty.

Until now.

Hallmark figured it out.

But one characteristic of this private company named Hallmark is humility. So, I was ecstatic to learn that this soft-spoken company that exemplifies the very best wished to share their emotion message with the rest of the business world—to help other companies achieve their own crowning edge. Perhaps I should not have been surprised. After all, what would you expect from the company that cares enough to send the very best?

I must share with you that after all my interviews and research for this book were completed, I arrived at a totally different, groundbreaking way of looking at marketing. Many would say it's just common sense. I think it's more. I call it "care sense."

Once you discover what Emotion Marketing is all about, I hope you care enough to make it true for your customers.

Vicki Lenz

PART ONE

Why Emotion Marketing Works

CHAPTER ONE

The Business Case for Emotion Marketing

What if you could add one element to your marketing strategy, and be confident it would differentiate your brand from the competition, make your customers more loyal, and ultimately increase profits?

What if that key element could enhance every aspect of your business—from the way you answer the phone to communications with your most important customers?

And what if it's something so simple—so fundamental—that it's been there all along, but you just haven't been able to harness its power?

The element is emotion. Not in its everyday sense—intangible, irrational, *mushy*—but as a force capable of inspiring customers to act. To buy. To stick around.

Hallmark Cards has built an enduring business on emotion. For more than 90 years people have trusted Hallmark with their most important relationships—relationships deeply rooted in emotional connections.

Business relationships aren't that different. Research indicates that strong satisfaction with a product or service, although a *prerequisite* for loyalty, doesn't guarantee committed customers. Something else is required—a bridge between satisfaction and loyalty.

"Emotion Marketing" is the enterprise-wide pursuit of a sustainable connection that makes customers feel so valued and cared for they'll go out of their way to be loyal.

> *Emotion Marketing principles lead to strategies that are almost impossible to replicate, providing a powerful competitive advantage.*

It elevates emotion to the strategic level, recognizing its importance in creating or strengthening a relevant brand identity and managing the consumers' experience.

Emotion Marketing encompasses every stage of the customer life cycle—from acquisition to activation, retention to reactivation. Hallmark Loyalty Marketing Group clients who have put Emotion Marketing principles to work have reported remarkable results.

"By understanding and leveraging the special emotional connection between QVC and its customers, Hallmark helped us create truly incremental business results," said QVC Vice President of Marketing Doug Rose. *"We have indisputable, empirical proof for the power of emotion."*

Successes from other clients include:

- A lead-generation program for a major insurance company produced 235 percent more referred leads than their control letter.
- An activation and usage program for a national credit card issuer garnered a response rate of 19 percent.
- A national auto service company saw a 1759 percent return on investment on a mailing to encourage repeat purchases—the 38 percent response rate to the Hallmark mailing was twice that of the control.
- Another major credit card issuer generated over 10,000 percent ROI for a collections program, recouping millions of dollars that otherwise would have been written off.

Joyce C. Hall: Leader and Visionary

Throughout *Emotion Marketing* are excerpts from *When You Care Enough* (published by Hallmark Cards, Inc., 1979), Hallmark founder Joyce Clyde Hall's informal reminiscences. He overcame poverty and a lack of a formal education to create Hallmark Cards—and to live the embodiment of the American Dream.

From 1910 until his death in 1982, J. C. Hall labored tirelessly at making his company synonymous with quality. Consumers responded to his efforts by making the greeting card company's slogan—"When You Care Enough to Send the Very Best"—one of the world's best-known and most trusted advertising statements.

Others warned "Mr. J. C.," as he was fondly called by those who worked with him, that greeting cards could never be advertised like other products. Nevertheless, Hall became the first greeting card publisher to advertise in national magazines and, later, on national radio. In the 1950s he launched the *Hallmark Hall of Fame*, America's longest running and most-honored dramatic television series. Its reputation for quality programming reflected Hall's belief that the "public was more interested in quality than some people in television realized."

Today the company J. C. Hall founded has grown into one of America's leading privately owned corporations. Within Hallmark's contemporary success can still be seen J. C. Hall's personal values of quality, hard work, and loyalty.

Emotion Marketing digs deeper into the ground broken by practitioners of points programs, frequency marketing, and "loyalty" programs. And best of all, Emotion Marketing principles lead to strategies so specific to individual businesses that they're almost impossible to replicate, providing a powerful competitive advantage.

EMOTION *IN* MARKETING

Using emotion in marketing isn't a new idea.

Advertising agencies have always known that tapping into an audiences' emotions—love, fear, pride, jealousy, pleasure—works. Think of the MasterCard campaign that compares the price of things like trips or autographed baseballs to the "Priceless" memories and moments they help create... American Express' stories of unlucky travelers who ignored the warning "Don't leave home without it"... Nike ads featuring cancer survivor Lance Armstrong... Michelin's reminder that "so much is riding on your tires." Not to mention Hallmark's commercials— ministories some viewers anticipate almost as much as the award-winning *Hallmark Hall of Fame* productions.

Ford Motor Co. in 1999 spent an estimated $10 million to air a two-minute showcase of its seven automobile brands around the globe on the same day. The commercial featured a war veteran riding in a Ford Mustang convertible in a homecoming parade, an Italian couple passionately embracing in front of a Volvo, and Japanese girls playing in cherry blossoms near a Mazda.

The vice president of global marketing for Ford explained, "We are serious about trying to understand people and their lives and their needs in an emotional way so we can design vehicles, products, and services they opt to choose."

He wants viewers to "come to the conclusion that Ford Motor Co. has a heart and soul and has the kind of people and products that people will want to get to know better."[1]

Creating Emotional Commercials

Kids write "Hallmark" on the back of cards they make for their parents. When friends hug—or get a little teary-eyed—it's a "Hallmark moment." And yes, people often do flip the card over to check for the Hallmark crown.

Hallmark's overwhelming recognition, and its place in popular culture, is due in no small part to its commercials, beloved ministories admittedly and unashamedly intended to tug at the heartstrings. But even the most sentimental ad isn't meant to be manipulative; Hallmark is honor-bound to communicate with its consumers with honesty and respect.

Every *Hallmark Hall of Fame* presentation showcases a number of longer-than-usual commercials designed to convey emotion through evocative storytelling. Whether it's a holiday ad featuring a sentimental family vignette, or a more contemporary portrayal of love at Valentine's Day, the universal and central theme is building relationships.

Two important ideals help Hallmark and its agencies create moving, memorable, and effective commercials:

Understand the customers and speak directly to their needs. Hallmark uses the Value Star^{SM}, a proprietary tool for assessing consumer priorities* to enhance the products and services customers are offered and the messages they receive.

Hold marketing communications to the same high standards as the products and services. Hallmark's creative product leadership initiatives are based on "12 Attributes of Compelling Product"—they include emotional intent,

*Discussed in detail beginning in Chapter 2.

originality, authenticity, passion, storytelling, memories, relevance, timeliness/timelessness, and craftsmanship. Advertising is created to the same standards.

Effectiveness is determined by quantitative *and* qualitative measures: Are sales up during that advertising period? Did the promotion drive traffic to retail outlets? Consumers also may be surveyed before and after the spots run to determine changes in attitude.

As with all advertising, the challenge is matching innovative creative work with results. Sassy grandmothers have to charm folks into stores. Sweet kids have to inspire their parents to tuck cards into their lunchboxes. And tearful good-byes have to convince families to send cards as well as pick up the phone.

Even the most emotionally charged, critically acclaimed commercial is meaningless unless it meets objectives.

Ordinary marketing can change the way a person feels about a company. But Emotion Marketing impels people to act on those feelings—and gives them a reason to go beyond a single purchase to long-term loyalty.

LOYALTY = PROFIT

Customer loyalty is vital to success for one very important reason: It's directly related to profit.

Much research has been done and many books have been written on customer loyalty. In *The Loyalty Effect,*[2] Frederick F. Reichheld reports that increased loyalty produces exciting profit results in businesses as varied as banking, publishing, life insurance, and industrial distribution. Retaining just five percent more customers can boost profits as much as 95 percent.

Harvard Business School experts studied leading companies including

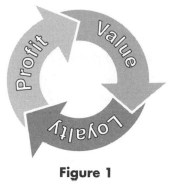

Figure 1

American Express, Southwest Airlines, Ritz-Carlton Hotel, and Intuit. In the resulting book, *The Service Profit Chain,* success and growth are shown to be dependent on the link among value, profit, and customer loyalty[3] (see Figure 1).

The cost of acquiring new customers is high and rising. Retaining customers is not only less expensive, but existing, loyal customers purchase more. They're more open to cross-selling. They generate positive word-of-mouth and referrals. And they're less likely to defect for bargains.

In short, increased customer loyalty is the single most important driver of long-term profitability.

In 1996, Hallmark teamed with Hunter Business Group[4] to conduct a nationwide loyalty assessment. Questionnaires reflecting the Harvard-identified dimensions of loyalty were sent to key marketing executives at the largest 200 companies nationwide in each of six industry segments—finance, hospitality, insurance, retail, transportation, and a catchall "general" category.

The "Profit and Growth" portion of the survey measured the bottom-line impact of customer loyalty efforts at the participating companies. Here's how businesses graded themselves (average scores from 320 respondents based on a top score of 100 percent):

77% Our organization is proactive in cultivating relationships with its best customers.

69% Our organization makes every effort to understand the reason for a customer's defection.

68% We know how much it costs to acquire and keep a customer.

65% Investments in cultivating active customers are tightly correlated to the expected return.

64% Specific programs and measures are in place to obtain referrals from our best customers.

61% We understand the total cost to our organization when a customer defects, and have programs in place to reduce defection.

60% Individual customers are tracked according to whether they are new, existing, active, or inactive, and marketed to accordingly.

54% Dormant customers are quickly identified and specific programs exist to reactivate them.

The results show that even customer-focused companies feel they have considerable room for improvement—they can't afford to be average when it comes to loyalty. That need for change is validated by consistently declining loyalty levels across the U.S. each year.

THE STATE OF CUSTOMER LOYALTY

So *why* aren't customers more loyal? A National Study of Customer Loyalty[5] conducted by Harte-Hanks Analytics in 1998 discovered the answer: *"The majority of Americans were willing to give loyalty, but the companies were not earning it."*

Customers have a high-level need to give loyalty—as human beings, we inherently need to feel connected with others, to *belong*. That over 70 percent of Americans question whether there is value in giving loyalty to *any* company clearly indicates something is missing in what businesses deliver compared to what they promise consumers. And that customers are defecting at unprecedented rates of 10 to 30 percent a year proves many companies haven't figured out what it takes to earn loyalty.

What would happen if you sold widgets, and at the end of the year discovered that 10 percent of your inventory was missing? After the panic attack, you'd launch an intensive search for the missing inventory. But many companies don't even notice the departure of previously loyal customers, much less recognize its effect on the bottom line.

Instead of addressing the deeper issue of earning loyalty, many companies aim no higher than measuring customer satisfaction. For customers, however, satisfaction is a given—merely satisfied customers don't become what best-selling business author Ken Blanchard calls "raving fans." They don't sing your praises. They don't commit for life. Not when they've got more information to base their decisions on and more options for meeting their needs than ever before.

So even total customer satisfaction doesn't guarantee loyalty but there is a connection. The National Study of Customer Loyalty, designed to assess every aspect of loyalty from the consumer perspective, incorporated the views of over 2000 nationally represented, creditworthy consumers across 18 industry categories. One of the key findings revealed.

> *Total satisfaction is virtually a prerequisite to achieving customer loyalty. Only a small percentage of Americans feel a sense of loyalty if they are not totally satisfied. However, the converse does not hold true. By no means does customer satisfaction guarantee customer loyalty.*

In today's customer-centric environment, product-centric companies often are startled to learn that even customers who indicate they are satisfied may be just waiting for a reason to defect. In one business-to-business survey, 65 percent of customers reported that they were either satisfied or very satisfied—with their *former* supplier. Simply satisfied, not loyal, they switched.

Twenty percent of American consumers say they are often or constantly annoyed with service and product quality; only four percent say they are delighted. *An oft-quoted survey on "why customers quit" found that 68 percent defect because of a company's attitude of indifference toward the customer.*

And one of the most common complaints in the National Study of Customer Loyalty was that new customers get the best deals—for example, 2.9 percent APR for the first six months with a credit card, or $100 checks to switch long-distance carriers.

In each case, the key to customers' behavior is their emotions.

WHY IT'S IMPORTANT TO CARE

The Wall Street Journal recently quoted a survey finding that "a surprising number of consumers say they act on their feelings about companies at the cash register."[6] When *USA Today* reported on customer frustration caused by the canceled flights that now seem status quo for the airline industry, one veteran business traveler summed up his assessment with, "I don't think they care about people anymore."[7]

> *The definition of Emotion Marketing includes making customers feel "cared for" . . . caring is essential to loyalty.*

The definition of Emotion Marketing includes making customers feel "cared for." There's an irrefutable business case for showing you care—as it turns out, caring is essential to loyalty.

The National Study of Customer Loyalty found "an extremely powerful relationship between caring and every key loyalty measure," adding, "Regardless of industry, when an individual strongly agrees that a company cares about them and satisfying their needs, levels of total satisfaction, strong company preference, loyalty, willingness to recommend, and willingness to go out of their way are also extremely high."

The study also found consistent and strong connections between the level of caring and future behavior intent across all industries: "Companies who are serious about increasing their level of customer loyalty should consider the importance of demonstrating to their customers that they care about them in satisfying their needs."

Working with Harte-Hanks, Hallmark initiated a follow-up to that study examining how four variables—caring, trust, length of patronage, and overall satisfaction—can help predict customer loyalty. *They found caring to be twice as important as any of the other three variables in predicting loyalty.*

The more a company shows they care, the more loyal customers appear to be. Just as in friendships, consistent demonstrations of caring build trust, encourage comfort, and eliminate the need for defenses, allowing a relationship to take place. Genuine caring allows consumers to lower their emotional guards. It produces the deep, fertile ground that allows a relationship to put down roots.

Caring is that bridge between satisfaction and loyalty. And Emotion Marketing is a proven, practical way to let customers know you genuinely care.

GIVING CUSTOMERS WHAT THEY NEED

"Understanding customer needs" topped a wish list for the year 2000 in a survey of chief financial officers.[8] Forty percent of CEOs surveyed in 1999 by the Conference Board cited customer loyalty as their top concern for the coming year.[9]

"Being 'customer-focused' is the mantra of businesses worldwide. But what does it really mean?" asked George Weathersby, President and CEO of American Management Association. "Successful companies know that being customer-focused means changing their point of view from seller to buyer, their point of reference from product characteristics to customer values, and their market-contact strategies from broadcast to one-to-one."[10]

In *Blur,* a book about the speed of change in the connected economy,[11] authors Stan Davis and Christopher Meyer write, "Human needs have changed little throughout our economic history, and are unlikely to change now. But the ways in which needs were traditionally fulfilled in the Industrial Era trained most of us to think in terms of products and services, and buyers and sellers. That is no way to think about the future."

Blur identifies speed, connectivity, and intangibles as the three change drivers for the future. *Speed* means businesses operate and change in real time. *Connectivity* ties everything electronically to everything else. *Intangibles* addresses economic value at work in the form of innovation, brands, trust, and relationships.

According to Davis and Meyer, "The difference between buyers and sellers blurs to the point where both are in a web of economic, information, and *emotional* exchange."

In a 21st century market that will hold few—if any—competitive advantages in terms of product or price, emotional engagement comprises a growing proportion of the value being exchanged.

> *In a 21st century market that will hold few competitive advantages in terms of product or price, emotional engagement comprises a growing proportion of the value being exchanged.*

EMOTION MARKETING: THE HALLMARK WAY

Emotion Marketing—this comprehensive means of adding value to customer relationships—has been a part of the Hallmark way from the beginning.

In 1910, J. C. Hall arrived in Kansas City, Missouri, with a shoe box full of postcards and single-handedly created the American social expression industry. At a time when the written word was the primary way family members and friends kept in touch over great distances, "Mr. J. C." instinctively understood the value of expressing emotion in building and maintaining relationships—both business and personal.

"When you care enough to send the very best" is one of the most recognized slogans in American business. Consumers trust Hallmark to help capture their emotions and share them with one another. It stands to reason, then, that Hallmark would be the natural trailblazer in the field of Emotion Marketing.

Through the ongoing practice, examination, and refinement of Emotion Marketing principles, Hallmark:

- Has built the largest active customer loyalty program in the world—the Gold Crown Card Program—with 12 million members.
- Consistently rates in the Top 10 in Equitrend's World Class Brands, and ranked fourth in the Top Ten Brands of the Nineties.[12]
- Is the greeting card industry's domestic market-share leader, selling over half of all greeting cards purchased in America. (Hallmark also publishes products in more than 30 languages and distributes them in more than 100 countries.)
- With 5,000 Hallmark Gold Crown stores, has the second largest specialty retail network in the United States (second only to Radio Shack).
- With consolidated net sales of $3.9 billion, ranks 29th on *Forbes* magazine's list of the largest privately held U.S. companies (1999).

Today, Hallmark is a multifaceted international company with interests in cable television, real estate, and retailing. Subsidiary Binney & Smith is the maker of Crayola crayons, Silly Putty, and other name brand products. Hallmark Entertainment is the world's leading producer and distributor of miniseries, television movies, and home videos. Since 1951 the *Hallmark Hall of Fame*—created to showcase high-quality programs on television—has won more Emmy awards than any other series.

PUTTING EMOTION MARKETING TO WORK

What makes a customer choose one company over another, time and time again? What turns your customers into your best salespeople? It's what many companies have overlooked: *delivering superior value.* And while most marketers agree that value is more than just price, few companies have attempted to understand the customer's perception of value, and how it affects their willingness to remain loyal.

> *Emotion Marketing helps businesses deliver the right emotional content and message, at the right place, at the right time, to the right consumers.*

Hallmark research into and application of the often overlooked, misunderstood, and underused element of emotion resulted in the creation of the proprietary Value Star^{SM}. Discussed in detail over the next few chapters, the Value Star^{SM} introduces a practical method of incorporating both rational and emotional components to generate a more complete value proposition for customers.

Using the Value Star^{SM} to develop an Emotion Marketing strategy helps businesses deliver the right emotional content and message, at the right place, at the right time, to the right consumers. Emotion Marketing has been proven to work across industries, for large and small businesses, in business-to-business as well as consumer markets.

Emotion Marketing is not a gimmick. It's not a new fad or a quick fix. And Emotion Marketing is not to be taken lightly, without belief and understanding, without ethics, without genuine care, and without true commitment by company leadership. An organization's ultimate purpose is to fulfill a specific role in society, and to meet specific consumers' needs. Profits allow further investment in achieving that purpose.

At Hallmark we believe in and practice the principles of Emotion Marketing, and feel a strong responsibility to share its ideals and methods. So throughout this book we'll provide case studies, tools, and ideas—all designed to help you meet *your* customers' most crucial needs.

And in doing that, you'll meet your *company's* most fundamental needs—to grow, to profit, to succeed.

TO SUM IT UP

- "Emotion Marketing" is the enterprisewide pursuit of a sustainable connection that makes customers feel so valued and cared for they'll go out of their way to be loyal.
- Ordinary marketing techniques, like advertising, may effect a short-term emotional response—Emotion Marketing inspires them to act and encourages them to go beyond a single purchase to long-term loyalty.
- The Harvard Business School's *Service Profit Chain* shows success and growth to be dependent on the link among value, profit, and customer loyalty.
- Overall satisfaction isn't enough to inspire loyalty—but it's a start, along with trust and length of patronage. *Caring* is at least twice as important as other variables in predicting loyalty.
- The future holds few to no competitive advantages for brands in terms of product or price—emotional engagement comprises a growing proportion of the value being exchanged.
- Delivering superior value to customers means more than just offering a desired benefit for a fair price—a complete value proposition incorporates both rational and emotional components.
- Emotion Marketing allows companies to deliver the right emotional content and message, at the right place, at the right time, to the right consumers.

CHAPTER TWO

The Value Star^{SM}—A Model for Emotion Marketing

To achieve sustainable profitability, a company must earn customer loyalty.

Realizing this, many companies have launched strategic initiatives like "loyalty programs" to gain advantage in their respective marketplaces. But in their haste to preempt competitors, they often overlook a critical in the Service Profit Chain: *value*.

It's not that companies aren't trying to add value. They improve products, add benefits, and lower prices—all according to the traditional value equation that assumes consumers weigh the benefits of a product or service against its cost.

But this conventional approach falls short.

Marketers find it more and more difficult to create value propositions that differentiate their brands from competitors'. Many ignore a more holistic view, failing to truly understand their customers' perception of value and how it affects their likelihood to remain loyal. And very few comprehend the powerful role emotion plays in defining value for most consumers and driving loyal behavior over time.[13]

The Value Star℠, the Emotional Es, and the Meaning of Life

The Value Star℠ didn't begin as the Value Star℠—it was simply an expanded version of a benefits divided by costs equation (product, equity, and experience vs. money and energy) based on customer feedback.

But as Hallmark's research department began to apply its new equation more broadly, the E words—Equity, Experience, and Energy—began to line up on one side with another E word: Emotion. And through continual application outside the initial study, researchers found it more useful to think in terms of creating value for customers by applying the Emotional Es.

When the Value Star℠ was born, Hallmark's research department took an evangelical approach to spreading it throughout the company. The new equation gave researchers a new mindset, which led to their asking different questions. Eventually it was showing up in other departments' presentations; internal businesses started talking about creating value holistically around the five key points.

This view required a bit of an attitude adjustment—some people tend to jump to "price" when they think about value. The Value Star℠ model represents value as a *combination* of Equity, Experience, Energy, Product, and Money. It acknowledges that different consumers value different points, so its use inherently requires a deeper understanding of the consumer base.

This made Hallmark a lot smarter about its research. Again, some of the questions changed: Were researchers dealing with a customer who valued the Hallmark brand? Or someone more concerned with price? Using the Value Star℠, they discovered ways to add value specific to different segments of their customer base.

Success in the marketplace depends on a company's ability to continuously create value based on consumer needs. One of the research department's early presentations was titled "The Meaning of Life." As the group put it, human beings—and companies—are on the planet to create value for others, which also end up creating value for themselves. After discussing their research, findings, and the Value Star^SM, they answered the question, "What is the meaning of life?" with, "To create value."

In a corporate context, applying the five points of the Value Star^SM provides a clear, actionable means to do just that (see Figure 2).

The classic challenge faced by all marketers is how to make their products or services more valuable to the consumer than those of the competition. What do people need? What moves them to act? And what influences cause them to consistently choose one product or service over another?

Confronted by that same challenge, Hallmark set out to determine what its customers valued. But instead of simply exploring ways to enhance the cost-benefit equation, Hallmark surveyed thousands of customers and asked them to define their needs in their own terms.

What emerged was a completely new kind of motivational framework. More discovery than invention, the Value Star^SM, depicted in Figure 2, incorporates the five factors that revealed themselves in the survey: Money, Product, Equity, Experience, and Energy.

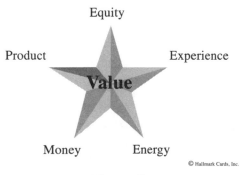

Equity

Product   Experience

Value

Money   Energy

© Hallmark Cards, Inc.

Figure 2

THE HALLMARK VALUE STAR℠

> *The Value Star℠ makes an important distinction— value has* rational *and* emotional *components.*

These five points further break down the traditional value equation: Cost (*Money* and *Energy*) and Benefit (*Product, Equity,* and *Experience*) still are present. More important, the Value Star℠ makes another distinction—it has *rational* and *emotional* components (see Figure 3).

The Rational Side of the Star

As Hallmark studied the implications of the Value Star℠ in more depth, the difference in the rational and emotional value drivers became clearer—and their significance became more obvious.

Money and Product are easy enough to understand. They're both rational—they're customer priorities based on logic and easy to explain. Is a product affordable? Is a service the least expensive? Are the desired features available? Will it get the job done? Is the promotion or discount compelling?

Unfortunately, if customers are buying a product or service based on price alone, the brand is at risk—unless it's the low cost provider and can sustain that advantage over the long term, a feat very few companies have successfully achieved. As soon as a competitor offers a comparable prod-

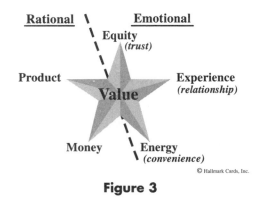

© Hallmark Cards, Inc.

Figure 3

22

uct or service at a similar or better price, any incentive to remain loyal disappears completely.

Even competition based on product is becoming more impracticable. Advantage is gained by offering *new* features, loading on *more* features, or getting to the market faster than the rest. When a feature is duplicated, the advantage disappears. As "fast-following" by competitors occurs more quickly, the duration of first-to-market advantages is growing shorter and shorter.

This isn't to say Price and Product are unimportant or irrelevant value drivers. Both are minimum criticals. *Competitive pricing and quality products are the costs of entry to today's market. Even the considerable power of emotion can't overcome an obviously inferior or unreasonably priced product.*

And obviously there's still benefit in improving the rational factors. At the least, companies should prevent them from becoming a competitive disadvantage. At best, an innovative product can be a strong differentiating factor in the overall value proposition.

But in the end Price and Product are simply too easy to replicate. Competing on price typically results in ever-shrinking margins. For example, when long-distance rates are down to pennies a minute and credit cards are offering low-single-digit APR, profits inevitably decline.

And continued reliance on these value drivers risks turning a product or service into a commodity. In many categories—long-distance service, shampoo, gasoline, credit cards, PCs, to name a few—there is little or no meaningful distinction between most choices.

The Emotional Es

In stark contrast to Money and Product are the other three value drivers— Equity, Experience, and Energy. Hallmark calls them the Emotional Es. And they not only provide opportunities for clear differentiation from the competition, but research shows they actually drive the majority of decisions to purchase.

> *The Emotional Es—Equity, Experience, and Energy—not only provide opportunities for clear differentiation from the competition, but research shows they actually drive the majority of decisions to purchase.*

Equity is a combination of the trust a brand earns and an identity that allows consumers to feel emotionally connected to it. A company makes a promise, consistently delivers, and over time its customers come to rely on it—simply seeing the logo or hearing the name tells them the product or service is worth the investment.

"Brands . . . come from shared experiences between the buyer and seller over time. Ongoing relationships build brands, not just high awareness of high-impact advertising," Don E. Schultz writes in *Marketing News*. "We found that brands are built primarily as a result of customer trust and reliability—reliability from the view of the customer, not the marketing organization. Brands are built on satisfactory experience by customers with the organization's products and services, and through their total experience with the entire organization, over time."[14]

For ten years Equitrend named the Top Ten quality brands based on a yearly consumer survey. Hallmark consistently ranks in the top ten—when it says, "When you care enough to send the very best," customers agree. Other brands singled out for world-class status include Craftsman Tools, Hallmark-owned Crayola, and Kodak.

The writers of an article on "Brand Zealots" in *Strategy & Business* recognize that "emotionally loyal consumers relate to the brand as they might to other human beings—feelings of affection, a common history, possibly a sense of trust and two-way commitment, which goes well beyond the satisfaction of a specific need. . . . As power retailing and the Internet slash consumers' search costs and competitors get better at quickly replicating innovations, creating value through stirring and satisfying customers' emotional needs is becoming increasingly important."[15]

The second Emotional E, Experience, deals with customers' interactions with a brand. Visits to a store or web site, employee contacts, communications, loyalty programs, and use of a product or service all affect a customer's attitude about the brand. In every encounter there's an opportunity to meet a need—and make an emotional connection.

Some companies create brand experiences so powerful they've become legends.

The Ritz-Carlton Hotel's commitment to creating an emotional experience is clearly spelled out in *The Credo:*

> The Ritz-Carlton Hotel is a
> place where the genuine care
> and comfort of our guests is
> our highest mission.
>
> We pledge to provide the finest
> personal service and facilities
> for our guests who will always
> enjoy a warm, relaxed, yet
> refined ambience.
>
> The Ritz-Carlton experience
> enlivens the senses, instills
> well-being, and fulfills even
> the unexpressed wishes
> and needs of our guests.[16]

From greeting guests by name to diligently tracking their preferences, Ritz-Carlton employees are empowered to do whatever it takes to ensure satisfaction. Their motto: "We Are Ladies and Gentlemen Serving Ladies and Gentlemen."

On a lighter note, the pure, unbridled fun of the FAO Schwarz experience is captured unforgettably in the movie *Big,* when Tom Hanks and Robert Loggia dance their way through "Heart and Soul" on the toy store's signature giant piano keyboard. A whimsical environment, entertaining employees, and the scope of the product offering have made FAO Schwarz a toy lovers' mecca.

The Internet has added an entirely new dimension to the idea of a customer experience. In *Sales & Marketing Management,* Dell Computer's Joe Marengi said, "Research shows that a positive customer experience drives more e-loyalty than traditional attributes like product selection or price. In fact, the top two drivers of e-loyalty are the quality of customer service and on-time delivery."[17]

The third Emotional E, Energy, is the investment of time and effort a customer makes in a product or service. Is it easy? Accessible? Worthwhile?

Again, the Internet has stormed the market—heightening competition especially in the area of Energy. Amazon.com leads the way with *1-click* ordering: Once customers log in and find a product, they're a single mouse-click away from having orders shipped to their doors.

Easy ordering is essential to online success, according to an article in *The Wall Street Journal.* "Some 60% of potential customers drop away with each additional click in the [online] order process," according to Forrester Research.[18]

Online shopping saves Energy in another way—by eliminating errands. Petopia.com's *Bottomless Bowl* lets pet owners keep the dog food, cat litter, and other necessities coming. Peapod.com delivers groceries on demand. Both save customers the extra step of reentering orders.

Energy means offering convenience as well as saving time. United Airlines has introduced a service that will inform customers by e-mail if their flight has been delayed or canceled.[19] Preregistered Hertz #1 Club Gold participants find their rental cars parked in a weather-protected space with the keys in the ignition; instead of having to wait in line and fill out forms, customers flash a driver's license at the exit gate.

VALUE AND BASIC HUMAN NEEDS

At the center of the one-to-one marketing phenomenon—database marketing, permission marketing, customer relationship management—is the quest to deliver individual value.

Value is determined on the consumer's terms in the context of his or her unique needs.[20] So understanding what needs make up an individual's value equation and how these needs drive them to act in a purchase decision is essential.

According to behavioral scientists, motives or basic human needs are at the root of all behavior. Regardless of gender, culture, or upbringing, there are common needs all people share.

In *Marketing to the Mind: Right Brain Strategies for Advertising and Marketing*, R. C. Maddock and R. L. Fulton arrange needs on a continuum from strongest (spiritual, personal, and physical) to weakest (circumstance, play, and time). As can be seen in Figure 4, *sthe stronger a need, the greater its influence on behavior.*[21]

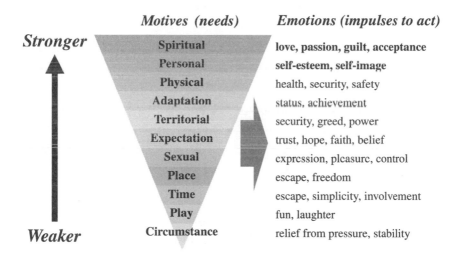

	Motives (needs)	*Emotions (impulses to act)*
Stronger	Spiritual	love, passion, guilt, acceptance
	Personal	self-esteem, self-image
	Physical	health, security, safety
	Adaptation	status, achievement
	Territorial	security, greed, power
	Expectation	trust, hope, faith, belief
	Sexual	expression, pleasure, control
	Place	escape, freedom
	Time	escape, simplicity, involvement
	Play	fun, laughter
Weaker	Circumstance	relief from pressure, stability

Data from: Madduck, Fulton *Marketing to the Mind*

Figure 4

> *To provide value, a company can associate its brand with helping a customer satisfy higher level needs. By meeting more than one need, it's possible to exponentially improve the chances of differentiating a company from its competition.*

To provide individual value, a company can associate its brand with helping a customer satisfy those higher level needs. And by meeting more than one need, it's possible to exponentially improve the chances of differentiating a company from its competition. For example, how about satisfying Play and Personal needs? The Disney Institute "combines enriching programs with fun and re-laxation."[22] Or quench a simple physiological need like thirst *and* enhance self-esteem, with a drink like Gatorade—marketed with the phrase, *Is it in you?*

EMOTION—BRIDGING NEEDS AND BEHAVIOR

Motives reside primarily in the unconscious mind, which makes them nearly impossible to fully understand or predict on a conscious level.[23] When the subconscious mind perceives an opportunity to meet a basic need, it stimulates emotion, which moves the body to act toward satisfying the need.

Because these emotions—or impulses—result in behavior, they serve as an important bridge in helping consumers identify their unconscious needs and take appropriate and immediate action to satisfy them. In his book *Emotional Intelligence,* Daniel Goleman defines emotion as "root impulses to act; the instant plans for handling life." The very root of the word emotion is the Latin verb *movere,* "to move."

Beyond bridging motivation and behavior, emotion also works in tandem with reason by bringing balance to the consumer's purchase decision process.[24] As depicted in Figure 5, the human mind can be thought of in two parts: one that thinks and one that feels. In most situations, both parts operate in harmony to help people navigate through life.

When passions surge, the emotional side holds the rational side captive, dominating the decision-making process. Emotions are hardwired directly to the body through a fast-track neural network—rational thinking is indirectly connected with the body's functioning.[25] In fact, emotions actually stimulate the mind 3000 times faster than regular thought. In many situations emotion moves a person to act well before the rational mind has had a chance to catch up.

Emotion also plays a part in more carefully considered decisions. Once a choice has been made, there is an emotional response to the final answer.

This explains why emotion is so powerful and persuasive in determining the outcome of many purchase decisions.

Take the decision to buy a new car. An advertisement might stimulate an immediate and passionate response. The rational side dictates the research process—checking the Internet for the Blue Book value, visiting dealerships, weighing options, looking into leasing or purchasing options. Then the Emotional Es come into play: What brand does

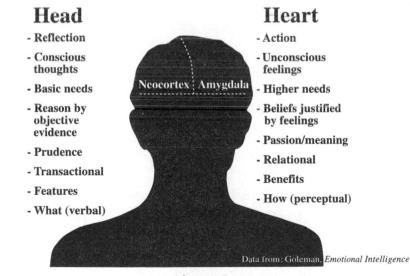

Head
- Reflection
- Conscious thoughts
- Basic needs
- Reason by objective evidence
- Prudence
- Transactional
- Features
- What (verbal)

Neocortex | Amygdala

Heart
- Action
- Unconscious feelings
- Higher needs
- Beliefs justified by feelings
- Passion/meaning
- Relational
- Benefits
- How (perceptual)

Data from: Goleman, *Emotional Intelligence*

Figure 5

the customer find appealing? Is the salesperson sincere and helpful? Does the dealership make the process easier? And the actual decision to purchase results in another powerful emotional response—from total satisfaction to buyer's remorse.

Saturn takes full advantage of the rational and emotional sides of the decision-making process. On paper, the cars have few advantages over others in their class. A *purely* rational analysis might not justify choosing a Saturn over, say, a Honda, Nissan, or Toyota. But it just takes a short visit to the local Saturn dealer or a brief discussion with a Saturn owner to understand why so many people choose Saturns. A pressure-free buying experience, impeccable post-purchase service, and a chance to join the dynamic "community" of owners are just a few of the emotional factors driving the purchase decision.

> *The answers to the marketing question, "How do we create a compelling, differentiated value proposition?" lie in understanding consumers' highest-level needs, and employing emotion to drive behavior.*

"The old paradigm held an ideal of reason freed of the pull of emotion," Goleman says. "The new paradigm urges us to harmonize head and heart."

Incorporating emotion into the value equation works because it's naturally how our thinking and feeling minds function. The answers to the marketing question, "How do we create a compelling, differentiated value proposition?" lie in understanding consumers' highest-level needs and employing emotion to drive behavior.

"One thousand years from now, little will be the same. But the emotions that connect us all will scarcely have changed" predicts a *Wall Street Journal* article on "The Engines of Life." According to Dr. Neil Busis, chief of the division of neurology at the University of Pittsburgh Medical Center–Shadyside Hospital, all of us have the same basic wiring with particular emotion triggers because of our genetic makeup and life experiences. "And if we are smart enough to understand the individual differences and use technology, we can set up mass customization options" to help people live healthier, freer lives.[26]

Decisions influenced by emotion are deeper and longer-lasting than those based on rational thought alone. Business relationships based on Money and Product will last as long as the purchase incentive exists—but once the promotion is over, or a competitor upgrades the product, the basis for the relationship is gone. But purchase habits based on higher motivations and emotional connections are hard to break.

Emotion is fertile new ground for marketers. As an element of the *entire* value proposition—not just the advertising—it's vastly underutilized.

"Future products will have to appeal to our hearts, not to our heads," according to *The Dream Society* by Rolf Jensen, director of The Copenhagen Institute for Future Studies, one of the world's largest future-oriented think tanks. "When this has happened, the prevailing societal model in the affluent countries will no longer be the Information Society, but the Dream Society. Now is the time to add emotional value to products and services."[27]

THE VALUE STAR^SM AT WORK

Using the Value Star^SM and focusing on the Emotional E—Hallmark is able to deliver superior value as defined by dramatically different customer segments. Over the years, Hallmark has become a leader in brand Equity. For customers who place the highest value on Experience, the Hallmark Gold Crown stores offer exclusive products, special services, and the Hallmark Gold Crown Card program. If Energy is more important, customers can find Hallmark products in mass channel outlets—or at Hallmark.com.

Hallmark has validated the Value Star^SM not only across different areas of its own complex business, but in a variety of other industries as well, including retail, financial services, telecommunications, and many more. In the Value Star^{SM}, Hallmark has discovered a practical, action-able framework for understanding, improving, and delivering a value proposition.

In response to that classic marketers' challenge, the Value Star^{SM} provides a means of understanding consumer motivations and using emotion to influ-ence their behavior. The following three chapters provide more detailed strategies for creating value by meeting consumers' requirements for Equity, Experience, and Energy.

Heading into the new millennium, all signs lead to a better under-standing of the individual. The battleground of the future is for the hearts and minds of each consumer. The winners will be those that provide a balanced value proposition by leveraging both rational and emotional benefits relevant to their customers. Only organizations willing to add emotional value can expect to achieve and sustain long-term competitive advantages.

TO SUM IT UP

- Emotion plays a powerful role in most consumers' perception of value and in driving long-term loyalty.
- The five points of the Hallmark Value Star^{SM} include ele-ments of the traditional value equation: cost (*Money, Energy*) and benefit (*Product, Equity, Experience*). But the Value Star^{SM} makes an important distinction between the *rational* compo-nents, *Money* and *Product,* and the Emotional Es: *Energy, Equity,* and *Experience.*
- Human beings share high-level spiritual, personal, and physi-cal needs—companies that can meet these deep-seated needs benefit from the strongest influences on customer behavior.
- Emotional impulses lead to action, bridging the gap between

consumers' unconscious needs and the behavior required to satisfy them. Emotion also works with—and sometimes overwhelms—reason in making purchase decisions.

- The Hallmark Value Star[SM] is a practical, actionable framework for understanding, improving, and delivering a value propo-sition based on meeting consumers' highest-level individual needs.

PART TWO

What Emotion Marketing Is All About

CHAPTER THREE

Emotional E: Equity

"The best metaphor for loyalty is really a relationship."

Claire Brand

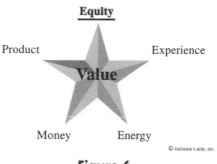

Figure 6

Harley-Davidson owners are rarely difficult to recognize.

Even after they've parked their motorcycles hundreds of feet away, your eyes are still drawn to their Harley-Davidson T-shirts and leather jackets or the Harley-Davidson toys their children (and future bikers) are carrying. If the weather's warm enough, they may even show off the most dramatic evidence of their brand loyalty—tattoos of the company logo permanently etched into their skin.

Harley-Davidson owners are perhaps the strongest—and most eye-catching—example of the power of brand equity in play. They're more than mere consumers; they are enthusiasts, perpetual advertisements. And they're frequently drawn to a community of other people like them called HOGs—the Harley Owners Group.

As soon as a good marketer spots Harley-Davidson owners, his or her marketing mind kicks in and wonders: What can my company do to ignite such a passionate response? How can I turn the people who *use* my product into people that enthusiastically *promote* my product? And while I probably can't coax my customers into a tattoo parlor, how can I get them to willingly and conspicuously display my brand?

Equity is the force driving passionate consumer behavior like the HOGs—and is the first of three Emotional Es on the Value Star^{SM}.

TRUST IS THE EMOTION OF BUSINESS

Equity is all about trust. In fact, the two are tied so closely together that a company simply won't achieve Equity without first earning trust. It's the same kind of comfort and familiarity that connects two friends, except in this case it's bonding a customer to a brand.

A company's foundation of trust doesn't appear overnight, but is established over time. It requires many positive deposits into consumers' emotional bank accounts. The good news is, once trust is earned, it becomes the foundational source from which relationships develop and flourish.

Before delving more deeply into Equity, it'll help to look at the role that branding plays in the relationship between a customer and company.

WHY BRANDS ARE SO IMPORTANT AND VALUABLE

The power of brand names can be divided into three progressive levels based on consumer perceptions.

Tracking Brand Equity

Understanding and protecting the level of trust customers place in the brand is of utmost importance to Hallmark, as it should be with every business. Because the vast majority of consumers recognize the Hallmark brand, the company faces some unique challenges in gauging Equity. A "brand tracker" increases understanding of a customer's emotional connection with Hallmark and how it translates to his or her behavior in the marketplace.

Brand awareness, brand preference, and *brand insistence* measure the different levels of loyalty to Hallmark. With virtually 100 percent brand recognition, awareness alone can't serve as a complete measure of Hallmark's equity. While awareness is an important first step, and a necessary condition for preference and insistence, it simply puts a brand within the consumer choice set, and isn't necessarily synonymous with strong equity.

Preference measures how often a brand is favored over competitors when given a choice. Research shows that most consumers prefer Hallmark to other brands of greeting cards; however, since Hallmark cards aren't sold in every channel, it's important to dig one level deeper.

Insistence is the strongest measure of equity. Customers are asked, "Do you *insist* on the Hallmark brand?" to discover whether they will go out of their way to make a purchase. It implies that no other brand will do.

For Hallmark, it's important to measure—and maintain—all three levels of loyalty.

Brand awareness. Some brands have a widely recognizable name that has risen above the media clutter, placing them within the set of options consumers consider. But without a compelling promotion or price break, people fall short of purchasing these brands. Companies like this still have a lot of growth to pursue.

Brand preference. There's a subset of recognizable brands made up of respected brands—names that consumers hold a positive opinion of. People may lean toward these brands among their choices, but won't go out of their way to purchase them. Preference is a competitive advantage, but doesn't fulfill the potential a strong name can deliver.

Brand insistence. Within preferred brands is the most exclusive subset—those products and services people *demand.* These names are trusted to such an extent that consumers are willing to pay a premium or go out of their way to find them. Nothing else will do.

The power behind a brand name that consumers insist on is undeniable. And it all begins with a promise—a promise to deliver value to consumers. If all goes well, it becomes a set of expectations. As those expectations are fulfilled again and again, a reputation develops. Consumers can eventually think so highly of a company that the business relationship begins to resemble a personal one. People come to rely on, seek out, and support brands much like they do certain friendships.

And just as it's impossible to put a price tag on the benefits of friendship, marketing organizations have struggled to find hard numbers to express the financial value of a brand name. How does one capture and quantify something so deeply rooted and all-encompassing as the halo effect of a successful company's name?

Powerful brands assert their strength at every phase of a customer relationship. They make it easier to:

J. C. Hall on Advertising for Brand Insistence

from *When You Care Enough,* published by Hallmark Cards, Inc., 1979

Advertising had always interested me. I pored over magazine ads when I was a boy working in my brothers' bookstore. And in the 1920s, when Americans started using greeting cards in greater numbers, I felt they should be told about the custom in some important way. We ran our first national ad, a full page I wrote myself, in the *Ladies' Home Journal* in 1928.

By the mid-thirties we started talking to advertising agencies about a program. None of them were enthusiastic, and a good many frankly said they were not even interested. The few willing to explore the idea said that our name and trademark would have to be on the front of the cards to make an advertising campaign pay off. This, of course, was unthinkable—people weren't buying advertisements, they were buying greeting cards. One agency head told me: "You'll never be able to advertise greeting cards if you expect people to turn them over and read the name." Another said: "Greeting cards can't be sold for a brand name like other products." And one man was more emphatic: "You can't afford to justify the expense of advertising." Our competitors felt the same way, as well as most of the people in our own organization.

After a discouraging time, I had lunch with the president of a small, progressive agency. He said that if our product and distribution were strong enough—compared to that of our competition—national advertising would be feasible. He believed that any product could be advertised successfully with this combination and the right agency. We experimented by advertising in one area, Chicago, where we had solid distribution.

The agency—Henri, Hurst and McDonald—recommended an established radio personality on WMAQ, Tony Wons, who chatted and read poems and quotations to his listeners. The format was a natural for greeting cards. In October 1938, *Tony Wons' Radio Scrapbook* went on the air three times a week. Tony talked informally and read sentiments from Hallmark cards—and at the end he would add, "Look on the back for the identifying mark—a Hallmark card."

A few weeks before Christmas, Tony received a letter from an elderly woman, Mary McDonnell, in the Cook County Nursing Home. She wrote that his show was one of the few pleasures she had in life—she was alone in the world and hoped Tony would send her a Christmas card.

It was typical of Tony to go out of his way to visit her. On his next program he referred to her as "Grandma McDonnell" and read her letter. He said he was going to send her a Christmas card and suggested his listeners do the same. More than twenty thousand people responded—not only with cards, but gifts as well, addressed to "Grandma McDonnell." A special room had to be set aside in the home to accommodate everything.

- acquire new customers
- retain and grow current customers
- cross-sell complementary products and services
- establish positive word-of-mouth and earn referrals
- fend off competitors
- win back defections

Take, for instance, Disney—a name that has staked out territory near the top of brand surveys for as long as they've been published. If pressed to calculate the value of the Disney name, the most obvious place to start is the comfort parents feel parting with a great deal of money to please their children with a Magic Kingdom vacation.

But looking beyond that, the value multiplies exponentially. Brand strength is also present in the same family's eagerness to try, sight unseen, a new Disney venture like a cruise or an animal park. It's present as the family passes up similar, even lower-priced vacations offered by competitors, and in their willingness to recommend Disney to friends and family. And the brand strength thrives at headquarters, too, where the promotions department spends less on advertising product extensions than it would if the brand name were weak.

As complicated as it is to measure the value of a brand name, one thing is certain: Trustworthy brands will continue gaining momentum as today's economy evolves. The Internet is expanding the number of product and service choices available. As it does, the amount of time consumers have to evaluate all these new options, strangely enough, is decreasing. Mix in the fact that advertisements are getting louder, splashier, more aggressive, and less avoidable, and the result is a consumer tendency to simplify buying decisions.

The effort it takes to research, experience, and evaluate many options is overwhelming compared to simply relying on a relationship that has passed the test of time—so often, the simplest choice is to go with a trusted brand.

> *Consumers can eventually think so highly of a company that the business relationship begins to resemble a personal one. People come to rely on, seek out, and support brands much like they do certain friendships.*

EQUITY: WHERE IDENTITY AND IMAGE MEET

A strong business relationship relies on two components: brand identity and brand image. While they may sound like the same thing, they're more like different sides of a single coin. Brand *identity* is what a company aspires to be. It's in the personality the company conveys, the decisions it makes, the messages it sends to consumers. Brand *image* is how consumers actually perceive the brand. It's in the opinions they form and the ways they interpret all the things a company does. *Simply put, Equity depends on how the company presents itself versus how consumers perceive it.*

When identity and image don't match, the result is a lack of clarity, rapport, and trust. And where there's no trust, there will be no Equity, since the two travel hand in hand.

A far better scenario is when brand identity and brand image *do* click—when customers accurately perceive what a company wants to be.

> *When identity and image don't match, the result is a lack of clarity, rapport, and trust. And where there's no trust, there will be no Equity, since the two travel hand in hand.*

In this case, a brand makes a promise to a consumer; the consumer tests it, believes it, and internalizes it. Identity and image overlap. They coincide. The company grows a solid reputation, and with it come trust and Equity.

Equity Starts with Identity

A company begins asserting an identity with its aspirations: What does it strive to be? What promises does it intend to deliver? Wal-Mart has identified itself as a low-price leader that's friendly, long on small-town values, distinctly pro-American, and a store that offers everything consumers need under one roof. The company has firmly planted these stakes in the ground and focuses on not straying from this personality. An identity that's not crisp enough will quickly confuse consumers.

In order to thrive, a brand identity has to be more than well-defined. It must be durable and timeless. It's got to have "legs." A company must not only communicate its message well, but communicate it consistently, across different media and consumer contact points. Do the web site, print ads, delivery people, and packaging speak uniformly? Ideally, yes. A solid brand constantly repeats its message and reinforces its personality.

Clearly, not all brand identities are created equal—there are many variables and factors in play. One single factor, though, is absolutely essential in separating the also-rans from the market leaders: emotion. Disney and Hallmark are good illustrations—two companies that learned very early that the most powerful, enduring brands will be rooted in emotion, addressing people's most basic, common needs, such as security, happiness, and love.

Disney excels in so many different industries because it's deliberately avoided defining itself too narrowly. Instead, Disney aspires to provide many different experiences, all with one thing in common: They're steeped in emotion. In a word, Disney wants to provide *magic*. Whether watching a Disney animated film or visiting a Disney theme park, it's very clear the company intends for every experience to be truly special.

When Hallmark leaders sat down to decide how they would define the company's personality and what the name should stand for, they identified eight qualities for Hallmark to embody:

- Creativity
- Caring/Loving
- Personal
- Elegance
- Tradition
- High Quality
- Emotion
- Great Value

The leaders also crafted a brand promise for its target customers: *Hallmark wants to be the very best at helping people express their feelings and strengthen the important relationships in their lives.*

The eight qualities and the brand promise became Hallmark's brand identity—the aspirations communicated to consumers, and the foundation around which the business is structured. While Hallmark remains very concerned about quality issues like paper stock and color reproduction, the brand identity is distinctly, and strategically, one of emotion.

Is it a coincidence that Hallmark and Disney consistently appear near the top of brand rankings? Probably not, because brand identities that successfully speak to human emotions are rewarded a sustainable competitive advantage. Once a company has identified its personality and message by leveraging emotion, a competitor will struggle to do the same without appearing less genuine. Compare this to the ease of matching another business's low price or copying a product feature—an emotional appeal is just too difficult to replicate.

It's interesting to watch other industries discover this ability to leverage emotion, particularly industries where at first glance an emotional appeal would seem like a disconnect. Take Michelin tires. Their most effective ad campaign doesn't even hint about the quality of rubber they use, how long their treads last, or how much their products cost. The simple image of a baby sitting contentedly in a tire, floating comfortably over wet pavement, packs enough emotional punch that Michelin doesn't have to say anything else. "We sell safety and security," they're telling consumers. "And we provide this peace of mind where it matters most—with your family."

MasterCard accomplishes perhaps an even more surprising feat: adding emotion to the highly competitive, mostly transactional, numbers-driven credit card industry. The cynical public that's grown skeptical and weary of credit card offers is the same public that's embraced MasterCard's "Priceless" campaign. Instead of purely fighting the price war, MasterCard has used emotion to insulate itself from the competitive fray. Its brand has graduated to a level all its own, where MasterCard is positioned not as a mere credit provider, but as a means to enjoy and share life's more emotional experiences.

Even the least marketing-savvy consumers can probably easily name another dozen clear brand identities. Chances are good that the first ones that come to mind also have strong emotional content—because *the most memorable and enduring brands not only linger in people's rational minds, they also creep into their emotional cores.*

In this emotional core, consumers form their opinions and make their purchase decisions. This is the place where all brands should strive to be.

Marrying Brand Image to Brand Identity

If brand identity sounds like a big chunk, it is—often involving high-powered consultants, off-site manager retreats, and lots of flip charts. Brand identity, however, is only half the story. After a company has defined what it aspires to be and communicated it consistently, the process falls to consumers to hear the message and experience the brand. They form opinions and perceptions. And these become the brand image.

This Hallmark Shoebox card in Figure 7 illustrates the point uniquely:

Figure 7

Needless to say, a business doesn't want this sort of disconnect with its brand. There's an image to think about and profits to consider. (And there may be a Hallmark humor artist waiting nearby with a sketchbook in hand.)

Once a company has devoted resources to developing a strong identity, it must strive to ensure that consumers perceive the brand accurately. Identity and image must coincide for trust to develop. That's how Equity is born.

Hallmark, for instance, has striven to establish a crisp brand identity: The company has positioned itself to be creative and caring, and its products high quality and personal. But what if a consumer walks into a Hallmark Gold Crown store expecting to buy an elegant greeting card with a caring message and instead finds the product vulgar or shoddy? The consumer would feel cheated on the brand promise, she'd make a withdrawal from her emotional bank account, and Hallmark would have an image problem. Trust would suffer, equity would disappear, and with them go profits.

Communicate Consistently with Every Customer Interaction

Fortunately, Hallmark attempts to communicate its identity to consumers *and* employees. All companies must purposefully take good care of the brand not only in the retail environment and advertising, but in-house as well. The result is a workforce that feels empowered to question decisions and keep brand identity in focus. Nordstrom has done a great job communicating its identity to its workforce. As a result, its employees are important allies in building Nordstrom's brand image—they've helped equate the brand name with strong customer service. Nordstrom nailed down their identity with a definitive rule, and trusts employees to follow through on it: *Use your good judgment in all situations.* As a result, salespeople will bend over backward to meet customers' questions and requests. Consumers come away with an image that matches the brand identity. And they feel a connection with the company, trusting Nordstrom to care about their needs.

All brands need to take this step—communicating their message not just to consumers, but to employees as well. In fact, every interaction that occurs between a company and its customers influences brand image and, in turn, Equity. With all the options available today, will consumers likely put their trust in a company whose products communicate one message, print ads another, and their support center something entirely different? Probably not. A company must align its identity with all its customer interactions. Things like:

- retail environment
- product and packaging
- web site
- direct mail and e-mail
- mass advertising (television, print, radio, outdoor)
- call center
- customer service reps

And on and on. A company must strenuously follow through with its brand identity and vigilantly execute its promises so consumers form an accurate perception. *The entire company must fixate on identity if the desired image is going to follow.* Once a positive brand image is established, there's a solid relationship built on trust. And a wealth of Equity awaiting those who succeed.

A Whole New Level: What Happens When Emotion Is Added to Equity

It's already been illustrated how Michelin and MasterCard used emotion to take their brand *identities* to new levels. But what about when brand *Equity* is based in emotion—when consumers complete the loop and trust the emotional promise a brand makes? The payoff can be phenomenal. Companies in this position have a remarkable relationship with their consumers, a connection they can rely on when introducing new products or fall back on during challenging times. Just as true friends will give each other a second or third chance when they make a mistake or fall short on a promise, so will customers.

Take Coca-Cola, a perennially successful and well-regarded brand whose ad campaigns have always made strong emotional appeals. Recently, Coca-Cola has been hit with several major challenges, none more serious than a breakout of illness in some Europeans after drinking its products.

Yet in an on-line survey reported by *The Wall Street Journal*[28] in which respondents evaluated the reputations of American companies, which brand scored the second highest ranking (along with Johnson & Johnson (1) and Hewlett-Packard (3))? Coca-Cola. Now *that's* Equity. While Coke responded swiftly to its challenges with sound public relations strategies and decisive action, its longstanding relationship with consumers provided the positive, trusting context for it all to play out successfully.

> *But what about when brand Equity is based in emotion— when consumers complete the loop and trust the emotional promise a brand makes? The payoff can be phenomenal.*

Across the six individual categories, many different brands rose to the top. But only the *emotional appeal* category led with the same three names as the overall survey. It was the best indicator of an overall brand reputation. Just more evidence of the strong correlation linking emotional appeal to Equity. Coca-Cola's consistently high brand rankings, year after year, in boom times and challenging ones, adds further proof.

ONE-TO-ONE MARKETING

Ideally, a company's strong reputation transcends differences in consumers. In reality, though, differences among people (both demographic and psychographic) influence their image of a brand name. Just because identity and image overlap within one group of people doesn't mean they do so for everyone.

A typical response to these differences is to segment target consumers into a few relevant clusters, then design brand identities and value propositions to fit each one. Car companies segment often, positioning distinct brands (or, in their case, *makes*) for widely different consumer groups. General Motors, for example, uses the Chevrolet name to introduce its vehicles to younger, moderate-income consumers. As these people grow, GM tries to retain them by offering more expensive, performance-driven Pontiacs. Ultimately, the automaker strives to earn such a high level of trust that when consumers are ready for a high-priced, high-profit luxury car, they turn to Cadillac.

Think of this progression in terms of the customer life cycle. Early on, when a consumer is in the Acquisition stage, a company delivers one set of promises and products. It gradually shifts the value proposition as these people become customers and move into other sequential stages like Assimilation and Retention. Different brand identities are naturally needed to appeal to different customer life stages and mindsets.

An important objective of Emotion Marketing is to drive this segmentation even further, all the way down to a personalized level. The most successful loyalty programs connect with customers on a one-to-one basis, reassuring each person that he or she is valued and recognized as an individual, not as someone who fits a demographic segment. In a perfectly built one-to-one marketing strategy, a company delivers a unique value proposition for each and every customer and nurtures individual relationships with them all.

Hallmark has found that even when a company is unable to develop personalized marketing strategies, it can still benefit by individually communicating to people with customized pieces. And the most important group to start with is, of course, best customers—a group that's already demonstrated it has loyalty to give. Examples of ways to individually touch a consumer include:

- Personalized notes recognizing a milestone or expressing thanks.
- Meaningful gifts or gestures not tied to purchase behavior, but that come "just because you're appreciated."
- Certificates for free merchandise or special privileges, especially if they're tailored to what the company knows the customer values and purchases. (Neiman Marcus, for example, offers private shopping nights for their best customers, sending a strong signal that these people have earned some exclusive extras.)

> *But marketers would do well by positioning as many offers as possible as pure emotional gestures—if people view an offer as a promotional tool or a bribe, the company risks damaging the relationship. . . .*

But marketers would do well by positioning as many offers as possible as pure emotional gestures—if people view an offer as a promotional tool or a bribe, the company risks damaging the relationship and causing a withdrawal from a person's emotional bank account.

An effective one-to-one marketing approach, on the other hand, shows a company cares—that it's taken the time to recognize and communicate to the customers who really mean the most. These same customers are eager to respond by giving emotion back to the company in the form of loyalty.

USING EMOTION AND EQUITY TO GROW

Another payoff of Equity is that people give companies permission to expand.

When people look for a new dentist or hair stylist, friends and family are the first place they go for recommendations. People are naturally more willing to accept somebody if he or she is introduced by someone they trust.

Relationships connecting businesses and consumers are very similar. If Equity and trust have been established, a company has the permission to introduce new products and services. Customers give successful brands the power to expand in other directions and further grow their business.

Several years earlier Hallmark conducted image tests to study how effective its identity was: Were consumers hearing the message Hallmark wanted them to hear? Did they trust the brand promises being made?

When Hallmark evaluated how consumers perceived its eight defining qualities—creativity, caring/loving, personal feel, elegance, tradition, high quality, emotion, great value—the company discovered it was winning in all areas but one: great value. The disconnect was contained to this one element, but nevertheless Hallmark had an image problem.

Gaps between image and identity can be very difficult to change. Consumer perceptions are not only held rationally, but can be very deeply entrenched emotionally as well. Hallmark knew it had an uphill battle—but also knew it had two important forces on its side: strong trust among target consumers, and employees who, like Nordstrom's, had heard an identity message consistently and were ready to act on it.

And thus, Hallmark's Warm Wishes card line was born. Warm Wishes is a line of 99-cent cards designed to appeal to a broad range of consumers. They are not positioned as "cheap cards," a message that would have hurt the other seven aspirational qualities. Instead the message is, "Hallmark provides great cards at a wide range of prices appropriate for whatever occasion or relationship you want to celebrate."

Hallmark's emotional equity came through for the company. People gave Hallmark permission to sell 99-cent cards as long as the cards were consistent with its brand identity. And consumers demonstrated that permission by buying the cards and delivering positive sales results. Since launching Warm Wishes, Hallmark has watched its market share increase significantly. Even its share of higher priced cards has gone up.

While Warm Wishes was Hallmark's largest product launch in years, it's only a single step in addressing the Equity gap regarding the company's desire to stand for "great value." The marketing and creative staffs continue to develop ways of solidifying this identity concern.

USING EQUITY TO STRETCH OUTSIDE AN INDUSTRY

This new Warm Wishes offering, though successful, was nevertheless just an extension *within* the existing greeting card category. Hallmark has also successfully launched products and services in entirely different industries, such as entertainment and home decor. This is evidence of the powerful emotional component embedded in the brand's Equity. When companies achieve this emotional breadth, they can take brand extensions into unexpected and amazingly profitable territory.

On the other hand, a business that has chosen a narrow brand identity (relying on, for instance, a product feature or pricing strategy to define its personality) will never be seen by consumers as having much breadth. Even if an image successfully matches an identity, the relationship will not necessarily be valid outside the product category, or at best, beyond the industry. Consumers simply will not trust a cookie maker to produce a reliable wristwatch.

However, *a company that has based their Equity on* emotion *can cross-sell dramatically different products and services to current customers and can attract new customers with relevant product launches.* Ultimately, if the products in a portfolio meet the same basic human need, consumers may not be confused at all when a brand jumps industries. In fact, they may be delighted.

For example, if Motel 6 began making children's movies, consumers wouldn't understand. The Motel 6 Equity lies firmly in offering low-priced, short-term accommodations for car travelers.

Then why is it that Disney, known initially for making children's cartoons and movies, can successfully operate hotels? Because the company has defined its brand using the language of very basic human emotions. Disney has elevated itself into the brand stratosphere by providing magical family experiences. Everything that falls into the emotional playing field Disney has claimed—and there's a lot that does—is fair game to pursue.

Now revisit the Harley-Davidson example. Its Equity does not revolve around spark plugs, miles to the gallon, or a no-haggle sales experience. Harley-Davidson has instead built a legendary success story by fulfilling basic emotional needs for adventure, freedom, and safe, honest rebellion. Harley-Davidson sells a lifestyle, and consumers have overwhelmingly given them permission to do so. That's why the company can stretch its brand name into product lines that at first seem unexpected—logo designed boots, jewelry, salt and pepper shakers—but are actually consistent with the Harley-Davidson lifestyle.

Ultimately, if the products in a portfolio meet the same basic human need, consumers may not be confused at all when a brand jumps industries. In fact, they may be delighted.

This consistency with brand personality is a critical variable when a company offers and positions new products. Hallmark's core business may be greeting cards, but the emotional promise that consumers trust the brand to fulfill grants Hallmark the ability to provide celebratory, relationship-building products like wrapping paper, party plates and napkins, gifts, photo albums, and more. Product categories that lack a strong connection to Hallmark's emotional identity are discontinued, sold off, or, better yet, never entered in the first place.

Like Disney and Harley-Davidson, Hallmark's relationship with consumers is emotional enough and strong enough that it can enter entirely separate industries. Hallmark's recent victories go well beyond a 99-cent greeting card line. For example, its family movies help bring people together and promote family relationships. *Hallmark Hall of Fame* productions have been accepted so enthusiastically that the company has produced more movies under the Hallmark Entertainment name. Films

J. C. Hall *on* the Hallmark Hall of Fame

from *When You Care Enough,* published by Hallmark Cards, Inc., 1979

I've been quoted a number of times as saying I don't worry about ratings. That's not altogether true. I do worry about ratings, but I worry more about the show. I'd rather hold the attention of twenty-five million people than just "reach" fifty million. And I've never believed that people who are watching your show are necessarily buying your products. The difference in our thinking is that we feel we need a combination of a good program, a good product, and a good rating to get good results.

We also insisted that our advertising reflect our slogan. When you are selling what is basically a social custom, it must be on a high level. People want to reach up for a social custom, not down. Our policy for commercials was a simple one—they had to be just as tasteful as the show itself. From the beginning, this eliminated singing commercials and silly or slapstick ones that are all too common on television. We were also opposed to a "hard sell" because people watching our show were our guests. After all, it's not how loudly you shout your commercials, but how good your programs are—and, of course, the quality of your products.

It may be that if more of the early sponsors of quality television had held out a little longer, they might have been agreeably surprised. At times in the early days we, too, had our doubts, but striving for excellence always prevailed. If we had followed "expert" advice or had let ratings alone dictate our planning or had been panicked by adverse criticism, we would have deserved all the obscurity that by now probably would have been ours.

Through the years we established standards for our shows: They must have importance and lend balance and diversity to the entire season. Classic plays, original plays, and long-run Broadway hits

> frequently appear on the *Hall of Fame* because they meet those standards. It took several years of experimenting to come up with a format for the *Hall of Fame* that satisfied us—and the public.

like *Gulliver's Travels, Merlin,* and *Alice in Wonderland* have all been consistent with the company's emotional identity and embraced by viewers in large numbers.

Amidst all these network broadcasts, consumers began asking Hallmark to provide its movies on videotape. Videos may differ greatly in format, pricing, and production from greeting cards, yet they fit cleanly within the brand identity—meeting a basic human need for strong family relationships. Hallmark responded to these consumer requests by first offering a handful of *Hall of Fame* titles in its card shops. Consumers loved the videos more than expected. The company has since made many more titles available, and customers have continued to respond.

None of these stories would have been possible—or even remotely considered by a marketing team—had Hallmark's identity been limited to greeting cards, Harley-Davidson to transportation, Disney to cartoons. All three companies decided to drill deeper than product format. They instead touched on what it means to be human, and the things people need to feel complete. There may not be a line item on any of these companies' profit-and-loss statements called "emotion," but rest assured—it's there. Emotion is present in every customer satisfied, every dollar earned, every financial goal for the future.

TO SUM IT UP

- Brand Equity is an enormously valuable asset and benefits all stages of a customer relationship, like acquisition, retention, cross-selling, and reactivation.

- Equity has two components:

    Brand identity is what a company strives to be: its aspirations, personality, consumer promises. Identity should be timeless and consistently communicated across all media and consumer interactions.

    Brand image is how consumers actually perceive the brand identity.

- If consumers perceive the brand name in the same way that the company intends, then identity matches image. A relationship based on trust develops and the company achieves Equity. A brand name will only gain Equity once it has earned trust.

- The strongest companies don't define their identity narrowly in terms of just a product or category, but as a source for meeting basic emotional needs, like: to belong, to be secure, to express oneself.

- Companies that have successfully established trust with their customers and have built their Equity around emotion have the permission to extend into new product lines, expand into new industries, and command price premiums.

CHAPTER FOUR

Emotional E: Experience

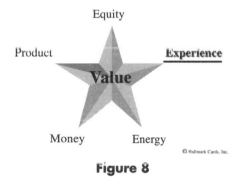

Equity

Product   Experience

Value

Money   Energy

© Hallmark Cards, Inc.

Figure 8

A couple of decades ago analysts for the movie theater industry greeted the launch of home video less than enthusiastically. Conventional wisdom suggested that as movie watching became more convenient, affordable, and accessible, fewer people would continue visiting theaters. Home video was the perfect solution to avoiding long ticket lines, sticky theater floors, and sharing an armrest with a stranger. Traditional movie theaters prepared for a shakedown and a thinning out of their industry.

But look around today. Communities actually have *more* movie screens than ever. Theater owners must frequently dedicate multiple screens to the most anticipated movie openings to ensure there are enough seats available. Granted, competition may be fierce, but one thing is certain: Ticket sales thrive. And yet—home videos do, too.

So why the dramatic shift in theater viability? And how could both categories succeed side by side? Because theater owners had to force their industry to evolve and redefine their value proposition. No longer do successful theaters consider themselves merely as film presenters. Now they provide a full movie-going *Experience*. The movie itself remains the central component to the whole event, but now it's enhanced by a number of extras. Theater owners installed wide, plush seats as comfortable as home recliners. They elevated concessions to a whole new level, upgrading their snacks and adding waiters and table service. New sound systems, bigger screens, prepaid tickets, gourmet coffees, more selections and showtimes, grand, ornate environments—theaters did more and more to distinguish themselves from the televisions in people's living rooms.

Think of nearly any industry, and chances are good it is or has been undergoing a dramatic transformation by the second Emotional E of the Value Star^{SM}: Experience.

WHAT EXPERIENCE IS

At first glance Experience appears to be an abstract concept—easy to illustrate, but difficult to define. But actually, there's an easy, clear way to think about it:

> *Experience is the collection of points at which companies and consumers exchange sensory stimuli, information, and emotion.*

These exchanges occur in the retail environment, at the point of consumption, in the follow-up stage, in *any* stage—even some that haven't been thought of yet.

These exchanges fall into three categories: (1) transactional exchanges, when the product or service is delivered and payment made; (2) informational exchanges, when rational data is shared; and (3) emotional exchanges or touchpoints, when the company and consumer connect emotionally.

For instance, when a person orders from a clothing catalog, a *transactional exchange* occurs. Getting the product specs is *informational.* Receiving an e-mail from a service representative making sure the customer's pleased with the purchase or getting a thank-you note from the company is an *emotional exchange or touchpoint.*

Companies create an overall compelling Experience for the customer by orchestrating each exchange so it resonates with the same pitch as the others. *The best Experiences are holistic, each exchange overlapping with and reflecting the others.*

Take credit card providers for example—they would be better served by structuring their acquisition, activation, and retention departments to align with each other. No matter how many exchanges take place, customers should always feel they are dealing with one single, well-oiled machine, not a series of distinct departments that follow different charters and don't even swap memos.

Hewlett-Packard is one company that recognizes the value of creating an Experience and maintaining a consistent tone through all its exchanges. The company identified "100 Points of Contact," ranging from the retail environment to the service support center to the repair person who visited a customer's home. Hewlett-Packard studied each exchange to ensure it fit into the overall customer experience the company wanted to deliver.

According to Emotion Marketing, a company that demonstrates this level of caring to its customers will be rewarded with their loyalty. Hewlett-Packard, no surprise, has found itself near the top of recent brand reputation surveys—no small feat for a player in a technology industry where priorities and business models shift rapidly and unpredictably.

WHY EXPERIENCE IS IMPORTANT

"The degree to which a company is able to deliver a desirable customer experience—and to use information technology, brands, and integrated communications and entertainment to do so—will largely determine its success in the global marketplace of the new millennium."

Bernd H. Schmitt
Experiential Marketing[29]

Any number of businesses can provide a satisfying product or service. As studies have shown, however, stopping at that point is not enough to keep customers long-term. A company must stir people's interest, excite them, turn them from satisfied shoppers into raving advocates. It must demonstrate it cares deeply enough to continually surprise them.

There's no better way to do this than creating an Experience that lets people interact with the company—interactions that engage people and allow them to enjoy the process. *Orchestrating an array of Experiences communicates that a company values customers and is eager to delight them and show just how important they are.*

Ritz-Carlton accomplishes this by giving its employees preference cards, an easy way for them to record when guests enjoyed something about their stay, then perform the same service during their next visit. If a visitor requests a feather pillow during one stay, then a feather pillow is waiting for them the next time, too. This level of responsiveness and caring inspires great stories and helps businesses rise above their competitors.

Take an auto repair client who recently told the story of receiving a random loaner car from his service dealer, and found that all the radio presets were already on his favorite stations. Lucky coincidence? No, just an alert repairman who checks presets in all his customers' cars then adjusts the loaners appropriately.

This kind of Experience elicits an immediate "Wow!" But an exchange this terrific goes on paying dividends down the road, because it

An Experience Just for Kids

Under several floors of manufacturing and office space at Hallmark's headquarters is the world's most unusual recycling center.

It's called Kaleidoscope, and it's a perfect place for kids to create, using paper, boxes, ribbons, bows, crayons, markers, die-cut shapes, and an ever-changing assortment of scraps from Hallmark's manufacturing process.

Don Hall had the idea for Kaleidoscope in the 1960s, and with the help of other Hallmarkers, turned his vision into an art studio on wheels that traveled to schools and community centers all over the United States. In 1975 a hometown Kaleidoscope grew up in Crown Center, the "city within a city" surrounding Hallmark's headquarters. Staffed by volunteers who assist, but never direct, it now attracts 85,000 young artists a year.

The Kaleidoscope environment was designed from the start to nurture kids' creative spirits. About five years ago it got a face-lift: A team of Hallmark artists was charged with creating bright, imaginative, larger-than-life sets and creation stations. Kids go to outer space to paint with melted fluorescent Crayola crayons that glow under black lights. A whimsical country house features a puzzle-making machine and a giant bug—little artists sit on its knees to make greeting cards.

In the Kaleidoscope world kids are always right—they can create whatever they want to, at their own pace, as their grown-ups watch from behind two-way glass (see Figure 9 on page 65). But to give parents a chance to play, Kaleidoscope also holds workshops—many with relationship themes. Some recent projects: Family Folk Art Quilts stitched from self-portraits created with fabric crayons, African-inspired Mud Cloth Paintings, and Family Celebration Chairs, decorated for special occasions.

> *This kind of Experience elicits an immediate 'Wow!' People remember this kind of treatment, make repeat visits based on it, and spread the story to their friends. The fact that the Experience made it into this book is noteworthy evidence of how quickly a powerful story can spread.*

definitely has staying power—"stickiness." People remember this kind of treatment, make repeat visits based on it, and spread the story to their friends. The fact that the Experience made it into this book is noteworthy evidence of how quickly a powerful story can spread.

Ritz-Carlton and this auto service dealer have used Experience to nurture relationships. They've delighted customers and created a whole new value proposition for them. In return, the payoffs go beyond tangible rewards like profit margins and repeat purchases. They include loyalty and legendary stories that customers pass on.

EXPERIENCE IN PRODUCT

The core of any Experience is the use of the product or service itself.

Some products are experiences in themselves: When you pay to attend a Broadway show, nobody is providing a product or delivering a service in the traditional sense. The good being exchanged *already* is an experience, something you watch, encounter, live through.

But every product and service contains some sort of experiential element in its use. Automakers, for instance, equip their luxury vehicles with a feature that remembers a driver's unique ergonomic preferences, so no matter how the seat, mirrors, and steering wheel get repositioned, a touch of a button returns them to the driver's preferences. Macintosh computers boast a friendly, personal interface that intuitively guides the user along while injecting some per-

Figure 9

sonality into the process. Surprising, compelling experiences like these are powerful forces because they add extra value and can be just the factor that moves customers from being aware of the brand to preferring it—even insisting upon it.

This idea of Experience in the product is important for low-priced, everyday goods as well as luxury items—with one significant difference. The goal of a product experience in a commodity is not to add luxurious extras; the goal instead is to ensure the experience is hassle-free, making it easy and convenient to consume the product. A simple, functional advantage like this is often needed to distinguish a brand name from the rest of the comparable, similarly priced options.

Consider something as common as potato chips. Some bags are sealed just right—tight enough to protect what's inside, but easy enough to open smoothly. Contrast that experience with the bag that makes consumers struggle to break the seal, then jerks open and lets chips fly everywhere. Experience also benefits a laundry detergent packaged to easily pour from and carry and beverages that come in aluminum cans with double-wide mouth openings. Every consumer consistently returns to a certain brand because of simple, experience-related enhancements like these.

Since all exchanges tie together, great products have secondary benefits as well: *A successful product experience will positively influence everything else that happens, setting a good context for the relationship between company and customer.* Wouldn't a company naturally have a stronger customer support experience when the product is great? And won't its retail environment be more enjoyable if the company doesn't have to hide what it's selling?

EXPERIENCE IN ENVIRONMENT

When companies address their overall experience, they tend to think first of the environment in which the product or service is made available— like a retail store, web site, fitness club, or doctor's office. After all, the environment is normally a customer's introduction to an overall Experience and the most visible, interactive exchange. Environment is also a relatively easy element to impact.

In the 1970s and '80s the Hard Rock Cafe revolutionized the way people think of eating out. By combining food service with a strong theme, it essentially created the category of restaurants now called "eatertainment." Customers, especially tourists, loved visiting Hard Rock Cafes, looking at the memorabilia, enjoying the music, and discovering the subtle ways the rock-and-roll theme played out in the restaurant details. Movie stars, supermodels, and professional athletes soon followed with their own theme-based restaurants. In fact, they followed and expanded so quickly that the market is now going through a shakeout.

But another factor beyond overexpansion contributes to consumers' waning interest in eatertainment: a lack of freshness in the environments. A family visits once and explores all the attractions. They visit again and the only differences may be the food they order or the location of the table. The family visits a third time, and, well—they may not visit a third time. Because repeat customers are greeted by the same, static environment.

The Sharper Image, on the other hand, has learned both the benefit of staging a compelling shopping experience *and* the necessity of revitalizing it regularly. The stores' products engage, surprise, and often excite the customer. The environment stirs something in shoppers that makes them long to try the merchandise—and The Sharper Image happily obliges, taking the product out of the boxes and encouraging shoppers to test it for themselves, to discover why they can't live without it. The company's buyers, who specialize in locating the most cutting-edge, technology-forward, unexpected product, help the store refresh its merchandise frequently and draw the consumer in.

Perhaps the ultimate illustration of a compelling environment experience isn't a store or a restaurant. It's an entire city: Las Vegas. When the gambling industry opened a little wider in the 1990s and casinos sprang up in state after state, analysts questioned Las Vegas's future: Would people continue to travel cross-country to use a slot machine if they could find gambling just an hour's drive away?

Like movie theaters facing a home video explosion, Las Vegas has redefined itself. The city has grown into more than a place to gamble. Las Vegas is now an *Experience*—on steroids. Sensory stimuli are blasted all over the Strip and beyond. Today, many people visit and bring their families, never intending to gamble, but instead simply wanting to experience reproductions of Paris, Manhattan, Venice, and ancient Egypt. The city doesn't compete anymore with smaller casinos all over the country; it has elevated itself to a higher plane.

Environment doesn't have to be this extensive—or expensive— to engage a customer. Just think of more visible examples from daily life: fitness clubs installing televisions near their equipment, car service centers adding doughnuts and coffee to their waiting rooms, furniture stores adding accessories and arranging their goods in miniliving areas instead of just lining up all the easy chairs against a wall. More inviting, fun, stimulating environments like these are popping up everywhere as business owners continue to realize that surroundings can provide entertainment, romance, intrigue—and a competitive advantage.

EXPERIENCE IN LOYALTY COMMUNICATIONS

"But experiences are not exclusively about entertainment; companies stage an experience whenever they engage customers in a personal, memorable way."

B. Joseph Pine II and James H. Gilmore
"Welcome to the Experience Economy"
Harvard Business Review[30]

Unfortunately for many companies new to these ideas, the pursuit of an engaging Experience often ends at the point of sale. But customers want more. Consumers yearn for—and give loyalty to—companies that extend and strengthen the relationship. This desire is at the very heart of Emotion Marketing. People want companies to consistently surprise and delight them *and* create an emotional bond. It's a tall order, but once that reputation has been established, consumers will work hard and go out of their way to stay loyal.

In other words, consumers are reserving their loyalty for companies that provide loyalty right back.

> *. . . consumers are reserving their loyalty for companies that provide loyalty right back.*

The best opportunity for a brand to make an impression on its customers is after the sale. And as previously noted, an out-of-the-ordinary exchange with customers, one that really "wows" them, makes a significant impression. Like the mechanic who presets radio stations, an unexpected note that's not tied to purchase behavior can really surprise a customer and help build repeat business and valuable word-of-mouth. Even more than the mechanic's gesture, however, these other touchpoints are based firmly in emotion, and are seen as special, relationship-building gestures, ones that begin to cement long-term loyalty.

The ultimate goal of using these touchpoints and creating a loyalty-building experience is to put up a fence around best customers. Being the first to foster an emotional relationship, following it up with genuine caring, and supplementing it with good sales messages that don't interfere with the emotion—these all help insulate customers from competitive offers. There's a strong parallel here to personal relationships—if a good friend and a distant acquaintance both ask a favor of the same person, it's pretty clear which one will get the person's time.

Building a loyalty Experience doesn't have to be complicated. Automobile dealers typically begin their follow-up process soon after a new car purchase. The salesperson may send a congratulations card to the new car owner, or call to see if the customer has any questions and remind the owner that the dealer is there for any needs. Saturn even sends a birthday card addressed to the car, celebrating its one-year purchase anniversary.

Experiences like these serve two functions: First, they head off "buyer's remorse," reinforcing the smart decision the customer made. Second, they strengthen loyalty via the emotional impact of a celebratory or supportive message.

Some companies administer points-based frequency programs as their effort to build loyalty. But these frequent buyer programs are different at a very basic level. They're purely transactional—one step down from emotional touchpoints—since the exchanges are only rational and informational in nature.

And while these systems may be a good part of a broader solution—and in some cases a competitive necessity—they've only been proven to *buy*

> *And while frequency programs may be a good part of a broader solution . . . they've only been proven to* buy *customer loyalty, not earn it. At that level, a company can lose the loyalty to the highest bidder just as easily as it gained it. . . .*

customer loyalty, not earn it. At that level, a company can lose the loyalty to the highest bidder just as easily as it gained it, since the relationship is purely utilitarian, without any genuine emotion supporting it. A company must provide the means for a customer to feel valued and appreciated, not bribed.

Hallmark has found that a company must recognize its customers *first* before setting up a points-based system. The sequence is critical. *Only after a company establishes a connection and demonstrates it truly values its customers will people let the reward program take root at an emotional level. Rewards then become a symbol of how much the company values its customers, not how many points they've accumulated.*

At face value, the Hallmark Gold Crown Card Program may seem like a standard points-driven system: Purchases earn points which are exchanged for merchandise. But the program has actually gone beyond that transactional level since its inception in 1992.

Hallmark's first loyalty effort was The Very Best Program and was designed to recognize Hallmark's top customers and fulfill their need to feel valued. A key message has always been to reaffirm the customers' commitment to relationships: "Since you communicate and appreciate the important people in your life, Hallmark feels you deserve some recognition all your own."

Back then the 3.5 million members were selected via self-reported behavior. They answered such questions as, "How many cards do you buy in a year?" and "How many do you buy in a card shop?" While Hallmark did give these members occasional certificates for free product, the gift was always positioned as a pure, appreciative gesture, not conditional on any money spent. Seven times a year Hallmark sent out a newsletter to the members, highlighting recipes, celebration tips, or ideas to enhance their relationships with family and friends. The newsletter also elicited ideas from Very Best members to reinforce their own emotional contributions.

The Very Best Program evolved, changed its name, and added a points-based reward component. But it remains steeped in emotion. Today's Hallmark Gold Crown Card Program continues to emphasize appreciation. It recognizes best customers and thanks them—even sends them birthday cards. It demonstrates appreciation and caring by giving away exclusive product samples without any quid pro quo or purchase requirements. And it still provides ideas, tips, and stories, helping these customers continue to enhance their relationships.

The result of these emotional touchpoints and informational transactions? Hallmark Gold Crown Card Program has grown into the largest loyalty program in the world, with more than 12 million *active* members. While many loyalty programs struggle to keep 50 percent of their members active, the Hallmark Gold Crown Card Program hovers around 75 percent. And Gold Crown Card members visit the store more often and spend more per visit than nonmembers.

The program succeeds in part because it fits seamlessly with other components of Hallmark's overall customer experience. Just as important, it provides the postpurchase exchanges customers hunger for. Many consumers visit or write their Gold Crown Store after receiving their birthday card just to thank the store manager for remembering them, saying it really made a difference.

EXPERIENCE IN CUSTOMER SERVICE AND SOCIAL EXCHANGE

The airline industry has seemed ripe for having one of its carriers step forward and identify itself as the provider of a great customer service experience. After all, other carriers are competing based on price and schedules. Consider also that the number of passengers, delays, and complaints are all rising at the industry level. And stories of "air rage"—an equally ugly cousin of road rage—are spreading as frustrated travelers argue with and even physically threaten each other or flight personnel.

Midwest Express airlines has responded, positioning itself as the airline that offers a compelling customer service experience.

Fliers know that Midwest Express is different the moment they step on one of their jets: first-class size, leather seats stretch the length of the plane. As they wait for takeoff, fliers are offered a choice of several newspapers. The food doesn't come in a box—flight attendants serve it on china and with linen, along with complementary wine or champagne. The meal is topped off with fresh chocolate chip cookies baked right in the cabin. Midwest Express stages a multisensory experience on every flight for competitive fares.

Many businesses, though, find it structurally difficult to stir the senses like this during their customer service experience. In these cases, employees make up the front lines of the relationship. Without the amenities of competitors like Midwest Express, Southwest Airlines relies heavily on its ground crew and flight personnel to create the customer service experience. Which is why Southwest hires approachable people with a sense of humor, then trains them to enhance the flights in ways their competitors don't. Flight personnel build rapport by dressing casually, leading songs, and telling funny stories during the trip.

If an Experience is the collection of exchanges between customer and company, then sales and service employees are the people accountable for representing the brand name. They are the faces and voices behind all social exchanges. They are the reason customers learn to trust a brand name—or decide to reject it. So a company must select them carefully and develop them completely.

What's at stake? *Studies show a positive correlation linking customer retention with customer perception that the company is accessible and cares about them. And a company is only as accessible and caring as its employees.*

Think of a local restaurant where the managers recognize best customers, call them by name, and know their favorite table. Or an insurance agent who really researches clients' needs and carries a wealth of client-specific information. The cost of abandoning the restaurant or switching insurance agents would simply not be worth losing the relationships or sacrificing the personal attention.

On the retail side, Borders Books and Music is one of many stores today hiring employees based on their enthusiasm for and knowledge of the merchandise. Their customer service and sales people heighten the shopping experience because they're able to talk in depth about books and music—and enjoy doing so. The employees' passion is contagious, creating an environment that elevates the product, even honors it. Bicycle shops, home improvement stores, video retailers, you name it—a sales staff can enhance the customer service experience by doing a better job of engaging customers' minds and exchanging more meaningful information.

Call centers often fulfill the back end of the customer service experience. This function has taken enormous steps forward recently by introducing high-tech *and* high-touch ideas to their systems. Powerful databases and customer-tracking software link critical personal information with purchase and service history. These tools help customer service agents access essential information immediately, answer many questions, and anticipate others. They can make personalized recommendations, provide on-the-spot advice, and advance the relationship with the customer. Hallmark has found that after the service call, an unexpected, handwritten note with a genuine signature can seal the relationship.

All these exchanges, especially if they integrate tightly with the rest of the overall customer experience, reassure a customer that the company is accessible and looks out for their best interest.

EXPERIENCE IN EVENTS

The story of Saturn's customer-appreciation experiences has been told and retold, cited and examined, many times during the 1990s—and with good reason. The "Saturn Experience" set a standard for creating a great customer experience by hosting newsworthy events. Saturn and its dealers have thrown chili dinners, conducted car maintenance workshops, and sponsored amusement park visits.

The 1994 Homecoming experience, however, is the ultimate of these events. It was a two-day gathering of Saturn owners at the Spring Hill, Tennessee, auto plant where the vehicles are manufactured. Marketers scheduled a variety of activities, plus the opportunity to bond with other Saturn enthusiasts and experience firsthand how the vehicles are made.

Saturn owners paid an admission price for the two-day celebration, but the company never positioned it or intended it to be a money maker. In fact, Saturn's invitation spelled out its motivation very clearly:

> *If you're wondering why we're holding such an event, the answer is this: we wanted to show our appreciation for the rather special relationship we have with our customers. And the Saturn Homecoming is the best way we could think of to give the people who drive our cars a chance to get to know the people who make and sell them—and vice versa.*[31]

Saturn may actually have been ahead of its time by charging admission for the event. Pine and Gilmore, in "Welcome to the Experience Economy," published in the *Harvard Business Review,* predict that someday many more experiences will be able to command a price on their own, independent of any extra products or services delivered. Visitors of The Sharper Image, Rainforest Café, or the local mall may value a heightened experience enough to gladly pay a cover charge.

Until then, Pine and Gilmore advise, companies should ask themselves, "How would we stage our own experience differently if we *were* to charge admission?" Saturn's Homecoming, for example, featured plant tours, food, children's entertainment, an arts and crafts fair, and a variety of concerts. Other companies will enjoy a competitive advantage if they, too, can infuse their events with features and encounters that delight the guests.

The Homecoming has become so legendary it's remarkable to think how quickly the company's customer loyalty caught fire. Saturn vehicles, after all, weren't available until 1990. Yet more than 40,000 people made the drive to Spring Hill, Tennessee, and tens of thousands of others visited smaller, local events. Like accelerating from 0 to 60 in a few seconds, the Saturn brand jumped from launch to national events sponsor within five years.

For almost 15 years Hallmark has been creating its own excitement for a special group of customers: the Hallmark Keepsake Ornament Collector's Club. The keepsake business nurtures the relationship with its 200,000 members by providing newsletters, exclusive ornaments, holiday cards, and member "surprises." Then, once a year, it pulls out all the stops and hosts a national series of events across different cities. Keepsake Ornament artists and staff members are on hand to sign merchandise, share food, and provide giveaways, demonstrating how accessible Hallmark and its employees are. Relationship-driven experiences excite these customers, who long for camaraderie with other collectors and are passionate about their ornaments.

Well-staged events are fun and entertaining experiences. But then again, so is a visit to an exciting retail environment like Virgin Records or The Sharper Image. Events distinguish themselves because they can be—and should be—pure, unconditional, and emotional. "The sale has been made," an event participant will likely think. "The company has my money, and yet they're *still* trying to connect with and entertain me." Over the years, businesses like Saturn and Hallmark Keepsakes have rented many party spaces and bought a lot of food—but they've legitimately *earned* customer enthusiasm and loyalty.

> *Events distinguish themselves because they can be—and should be—pure, unconditional, and emotional. "The sale has been made," an event participant will likely think. "The company has my money, and yet they're still trying to connect with and entertain me."*

RAISING THE STAKES WITH EMOTION

"The most affective experiences are the most effective experiences."

Paul Treacy

Think for a minute about a home computer. Studies have shown that the monitors tax the eyes and are detrimental to vision. Great sound quality is only slowly becoming available. Extended periods of sitting at a keyboard strain the hands, forearms, and back. And while computers may someday be able to transmit fragrances electronically, that's still a long way off.

Why then—despite computers' frequent assault on our senses—are chat rooms and online communities thriving? *Because the human need to belong and to create camaraderie trumps any physical discomfort or sensory stimulus.* There are different levels of impact that experiences make on people, and companies must learn them.

Experiences that trigger the senses entertain, though the effects fade as new stimuli arrive.

Experiences that engage the mind inform and satisfy, but their impact diminishes as thoughts move on to something else.

The most compelling Experiences, though, are emotionally affective— they may pause at the sensory and rational levels, but they eventually touch the heart and linger there.

All people are driven by a collection of human needs, such as to belong, to be happy, and to feel secure. Legendary customer experiences capitalize on motives like this. They take emotion and dial it up—way up—delivering experiences that truly impact people, and maybe even change them along the way. Companies should remember to emotionally reach out to their customers—for those that focus solely on rewarding them will miss out on being rewarded *by* them. *Consumers have loyalty to give. Rewards may rent their loyalty temporarily, but emotion-based experiences will* own *it.*

Hallmark strives to design an Experience that taps into these universal motivations. The goal of Hallmark's Gold Crown Card Program is to fulfill customers' needs to enhance relationships and feel appreciated. The Hallmark Keepsake Collectors Club gives members the chance to belong and be recognized.

There's another great example, though, that arrived somewhat unexpectedly, but with phenomenal results.

It would have been hard to believe 10 or 20 years ago that some of the most amazingly moving touchpoints would come from a shoe manufacturer, that a company focusing on something as unromantic as our feet would conquer consumers' emotions as effectively as anyone.

Yet in the last decade or so Nike has done just that. Instead of focusing purely on product features or athlete endorsements, the company has chosen an appeal to our emotional needs. The overall Nike Experience inspires people to compete, grow, and succeed. The motivational line "Just Do It" drove customers not only to purchase athletic shoes—it pushed people to examine their lifestyle and reignite their own inner fire.

Nike executed riveting ad campaigns that sometimes featured product, sometimes didn't. Interchanging humorous and inspirational approaches, the ads moved people and grabbed their attention. Consumers didn't just view the commercials, they internalized and talked about them—and they let the ads change them. When Nike recently integrated the television spots with their web site, the company elevated the ads to an even stronger Experience.

Nike stages experiences that are even more personal and interactive at their Niketown flagship stores, like the location on Michigan Avenue

> *Companies should remember to emotionally reach out to their customers—for those that focus solely on rewarding them will miss out on being rewarded by them. Consumers have loyalty to give. Rewards may rent their loyalty temporarily, but emotion-based experiences will own it.*

in Chicago. It's a stretch to call it a store, since selling merchandise seems secondary. The site is more like a monument to fitness, inspiration, and the human drive to succeed. Experiencing this environment surprises the eyes, ears, and fingertips. It engages the mind with fitness information and sports history, and stirs the heart with inspirational media and stories of human accomplishment.

These sensory, rational, and emotional exchanges layer on top of one another and come together with remarkably moving results. No wonder people have responded so enthusiastically to Niketown. When Nike made the environment a portal into the human experience, Chicago tourists made it one of the city's most popular tourist destinations.

TO SUM IT UP

- Experience is made up of all the points at which companies and consumers exchange sensory stimuli, information, and emotion.
- These exchanges can be divided into three types: (1) *transactional exchanges,* when the product or service is actually delivered and the payment is made; (2) *informational exchanges,* when rational data is shared; and (3) *emotional exchanges* or *touchpoints,* where company and consumer connect emotionally.
- Companies should orchestrate each component of the Experience so they all align with each other. Components include the retail environment, the product or service itself, loyalty-building follow-ups, customer service and social exchanges, and events.
- Points-based frequency programs are not enough because they're based on rational information and rewards, not emotion. A company must first recognize and value its customers, connecting with them emotionally *before* it rewards them.
- The strongest, most compelling experiences address an emotion. If experiences can meet people's basic human needs, then consumers will reward the company with loyalty.

CHAPTER FIVE

Emotional E: Energy

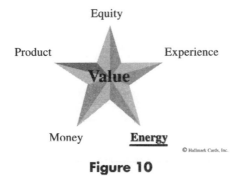

Equity

Product   Experience

Value

Money   **Energy**

© Hallmark Cards, Inc.

Figure 10

Over the last couple decades, as many American women have split time between home and work, as more men have picked up domestic responsibility, and as technology has progressed at lightning speed, grocery stores have transformed themselves dramatically.

They now have video stores, dry cleaners, and bank branches inside. Bar code scanners perform the work checkout employees used to do with their fingers and a cash register. Prepared meals are more available. Credit and debit cards are welcome. Salads even come in a *bag*.

A few years from now shoppers will likely use a single-step checkout process, running their whole cart through a more sophisticated scanner instead of removing items one by one. And that's only if they choose to go outside to shop in the first place. Today, web grocers like Peapod.com and Webvan.com can do all of a family's shopping for them *and* provide flexible home delivery.

Businesses that wisely fixate on conserving their customers' time are capitalizing on the third Emotional E of the Value Star^{SM}: Energy. Because Energy is all about time and its increasingly precious nature. Whether making a product or service more accessible, easier, or faster, a company is saving people's time. Though frequently overlooked, Energy is a critical piece of a company's value proposition.

. . . companies that waste people's time and Energy send the message that they don't care. The result? Customers make withdrawals from their emotional bank accounts. Or worse, they simply check out of the relationship altogether.

WHY ENERGY IS IMPORTANT

At first glance Energy may not appear to have the strong emotional ties that Equity and Experience have—but it does. *Companies that demonstrate concern about people's time strengthen the connection they share. They elevate emotion to the strategic level, strengthening the relationship with their customers.*

On the other hand, companies that waste people's time and Energy send the message that they don't care. The result? Customers make withdrawals from their emotional bank accounts. Or worse, they simply check out of the relationship altogether.

Time is the new currency.

In today's society, where information comes faster than ever and all deadlines are urgent, people feel their time is under constant pressure. Yet, strangely enough, we continue to try and fit more into our days. Many people find that the best solution is to prioritize—to recognize what's most important in life and protect the time spent there. As a result, consumers have shifted their thinking. Society is in a phase of paring down and simplifying, allocating time to the people, activities, and events that mean the most.

Marketers who can make all aspects of their product (the sale, delivery, use, service, etc.) as efficient and easy as possible give customers the freedom to spend their time on what's important to them. A single mother working a full time job, for example, appreciates the ability to do her banking online or at 24-hour ATMs located within other stores or at her workplace, so she can be home when her kids return from school. Consumers feel a connection with companies that redirect time away from transactional details and toward emotional commitments.

A business that maximizes people's Energy also sends the important message that it values its customers. Such a company demonstrates that it understands their priorities and wants to help them manage their time and Energy.

The consumer, in return, feels this emotional bond and grows eager to give loyalty back to companies that show they care. These companies are then in the ideal position to charge a price premium (knowing their loyal customers are less likely to defect for bargains), allowing them to focus even more resources on improving their value proposition.

HOW TO IMPACT ENERGY

Making products or services faster is not the only option companies have to save their customers time. Here are some to consider:

Saving Energy with Gift Bags

Twenty years ago, gift-giving required more Energy than just finding the perfect present. Consumers were perfectly happy to invest the time and money in gift wrapping and all that went with it—ribbons, bows, gift tags, and tape. Today it's not at all uncommon to hear about people wrapping gifts in their car on the way to parties.

In the early '80s, Hallmark entered the gift bag business as an experiment to discover whether people were willing to put gifts in something as seemingly simple as a paper bag. Sales proved they were—and now consumers name convenience as the number one factor in selecting gift wrap. Brand, design, and price are all important, but definitely secondary.

Gift bags let anyone create an attractive present—in seconds. There's no skill required, no box to find, no awkward tucking and folding and taping. But convenience means more to customers than just a fast- and easy-to-use product. Other Energy drivers include the channel (discount outlets and drugstores top the list) and the merchandising. For shoppers in a hurry, even displays organized by occasion aren't quick enough reads; they prefer gift wrap organized by format, with bags, rolls of paper, bows, and other accessories separated into sections. And today's gift-givers want pricing that allows them to stock up on supplies, so they always have quick and easy solutions on hand.

To keep gift-givers happy, Hallmark now targets gift bags at specific needs: low-price, all-purpose, broad-appeal bags for stockpiling; a broader range of designs, including licensed properties and occasions, such as baby, wedding, and birthday; and innovative designs, materials, and processes.

An attempt to really "attack" the Energy part of the Value Star^{SM} created a popular new approach that is now a customer mainstay.

Hallmark continues to rethink its approach to gift wrap, seeking new ways to differentiate products from the competition and to anticipate customers' needs and exceed their expectations.

Make Things More Accessible

The most obvious solutions are for companies to offer their products and services at more locations or through multiple channels: restaurant chains operating smaller sites inside mass merchandise stores like Wal-Mart; retail shops opening in airports; and ATMs strategically placed where people need cash fast and unpredictably (sports venues, nightclubs, malls).

But accessibility is much broader than this: It's also giving consumers the ability to make purchases *where*ver, *when*ever and *how*ever they want. Services like dry cleaners and pharmacies extend their hours to help attract people working long days. Books on audiotape make information and entertainment accessible while people travel. QVC viewers can shop the cable channel any time of day or night and can order products even after the program moves on to other merchandise. The company also provides a variety of ordering options: a live representative, the QVC web site, or a fast, convenient, automated phone system.

E-tailers have promoted accessibility by letting consumers shop 24/7 then delivering products right to the doorstep. Shoppers may never again have to worry about working around a store's open times. Some retailers like Williams Sonoma and J. Crew have done even better, expanding their products across the three most powerful channels—web site, catalog, and traditional storefront. They provide consumers the most choices of all, letting them decide for themselves which outlet offers the best solution.

Make Things Easier

Businesses that can take over steps from the customer—or take steps *out* altogether—save people's time by giving them less to do. Gas stations let customers pay at the pump. Online auction sites like eBay bring together buyers and sellers. Other companies make things easier by saving travel time and effort.

Mail Boxes Etc., for instance, sells tape, boxes, padding, and anything else needed to prepare and ship a package. Their employees are equipped with information on different shipping options so customers can compare cost, speed, and delivery days. In addition, these locations double as scheduled stops for major shippers.

Of course, Internet sites have been the leaders in making things faster by making them easier. But even their successes have not been without missteps along the way, and there's still room for improvement. E-tailers learned early on how quickly shoppers abandon their site if the interface is too confusing to navigate or if there are too many steps to the ordering process. The best web stores today design their sites to minimize the number of "clicks" required to complete an order and store repetitive information like a customer's billing address and credit card number.

Customers unsatisfied with their merchandise find the return process still developing. It takes a lot of effort, time, and money to repackage a product, mail it back to the e-tailer, and get reimbursed. Companies that have both web sites and traditional retail outlets ("clicks-and-mortar" businesses) are winning the Energy race right now by offering customers the chance to return web-purchased merchandise to an actual store. They can walk out in just a few minutes with exactly what they want and don't have to worry about a trip to the post office or shipping costs.

Make Things Worthwhile

An extraordinarily strong product or service gives consumers the confidence that once they make a purchase, they won't waste any more Energy on it. There will be no need to fix, return, or replace it, because the company will far exceed expectations.

Nordstrom makes their shopping experience worthwhile with merchandise and service that lead the industry. When Nordstrom customers make a purchase, they know they won't go home disappointed. And on the off-chance a purchase falls below expectations, customers trust the company will do what's necessary to fix the situation.

This making-it-worthwhile philosophy also drives "category killer" retail businesses. Their strategy is to fill their stores with every imaginable version within a product format—be it different brands, sizes, titles, makes, styles, patterns, or models—and to ensure merchandise is always in stock. Think of Barnes and Noble (books), Circuit City (electronics), or Bed, Bath and Beyond (linens)—if they fill their shelves with every option a customer could ever want, there's less chance the customer will leave empty-handed. Shoppers trust they won't have to visit several stores to find what they need.

Make Things Personalized

A customized solution or process is impressive to consumers. They can home in on what's *right* for them and avoid sifting through everything that's *not*. Personalization also has the benefit of making consumers feel more valued; after all, the company is speaking directly to them—perhaps even using their names—and providing what's uniquely important to their lives.

Not surprisingly, technology is a critical enabler of customization. United Airlines uses its web site to administer a flight paging program. Customers can visit UAL.com, provide information about their flights and identify how they prefer to be reached—alphanumeric pager, e-mail, or cell phone with text messaging. United will respond by notifying them of flight delays, cancellations, and gate information.

Hallmark takes its company's promise—to help consumers stay connected with the most important people in their lives—and extends it electronically at Hallmark.com, adding personalized Energy-saving features. Customers can register on the web site to set up their own address book, celebration planning calendar, and messaging service to remind them of important dates coming up.

Leverage Information and Technology

Making things accessible, easier, personalized, and worthwhile are great ways to give customers back some Energy. But what if there were a way to go even further—to not only give them extra time, but provide them the capacity to create even more of it?

> *... what if there were a way to go even further—to not only give customers extra time, but provide them the capacity to create even more of it?*

Information and technology do just that. Typically working in concert, they save consumers' Energy and enable them to generate more of it for themselves.

Online agents like MySimon.com empower people with information, yet simplify it enough so it's not overwhelming. MySimon.com is a destination for Internet shoppers to easily browse dozens of different e-tailers with just a few clicks. A user identifies the category of merchandise he or she wants to purchase, and MySimon goes to work, searching online stores for information, pulling together everything that matches the shoppers' criteria, and presenting it sorted by price or manufacturer. Other online agents perform the same service for travel and insurance, among other things.

Even if companies don't have sophisticated technology, they likely do have information from which customers can benefit. Sharing it will engage people and help promote an atmosphere of trust, empowerment, and loyalty.

Provide Security

A significant hurdle to using technology and information to their full potential is security. Many Internet users harbor doubts about the privacy of their personal and credit information, leading them to drop out of the process before they make a purchase. A company in this position must work hard to connect with people, earn their trust, and clearly define privacy policies to calm any angst. Security, in this case, becomes a critical factor in building Energy.

No matter what approach a company takes, guiding customers through an unemotional, transactional process more quickly means they are left with more Energy.

But Energy is not the end benefit a time-saving experience delivers to people. The end benefit is that customers are able to enjoy a relaxed family dinner, or go out on a date, or perhaps pursue a favorite hobby. *Whatever the activity, marketers need to focus on giving consumers the extra time and helping them fulfill their emotional needs.*

Emotion Marketers know the power of making things easy and delighting people in this way. While customers may not have the time to fill out paperwork or stand in line, they do have time to tell stories about which companies have saved them Energy. And they have the loyalty to return to those same companies again in the future.

> *While customers may not have the time to fill out paperwork or stand in line, they do have time to tell stories about which companies have saved them Energy.*

THE HERTZ VALUE PROPOSITION

Hertz Rent A Car has stepped back and analyzed how their processes impact Energy, and has done a noteworthy job pulling together different time-saving devices and strategies into a more pleasant customer Experience.

Time never seems more precious than when you're traveling. On vacation, people want to arrive at their destinations fast; on business trips, they want to *leave* their destinations even faster. Hertz has recognized this and responded with some noteworthy time- and Energy-saving components to its car rental experience.

Hertz created its Gold program to help its best customers speed through the rental and return processes, relying heavily on technology to cut out steps. The company already has all its frequent travelers' information loaded into its system and their signatures on file, allowing Hertz agents to take reservations more quickly and other employees to prepare the car in advance. At the pickup point, Gold customers can skip past the rental counter and head directly to the lot where big, easy-to-read light boards display drivers' names and corresponding parking spot numbers where their car awaits. The contract is inside, the keys are in the ignition, and the customers—feeling more valued, special, and grateful than ever—are off to their destinations.

The return process offered another opportunity for Hertz to marshal its technological resources and effectively manage people's Energy. When Gold members bring back their cars, they drive into the Hertz lot—no designated spaces to locate this time—and are met by a company employee who loads the data (return date and mileage, for example) into a handheld computer. A receipt is printed and the customer is free again.

Hertz designs each step to relieve Gold customers of any extra Energy burdens. The experience not only saves the customer time, but also leaves behind an emotional punch. Frequent customers are well aware that they skip many of the steps non-Gold drivers have to face. In fact, often as they head for their waiting car, Gold members actually walk past the other customers standing at the counter. This injects a feeling of exclusivity into the process. "I must really be valuable to Hertz," Gold customers tell themselves, "if the company is willing to make my day this easy." Seeing their names big and bright on a light board enhances the feeling.

As a result of all these strategic efforts, Hertz is able to price its services above the competition even though many other agencies offer comparable cars. The company can move forward, confident that the extra attention paid to Energy has earned customer loyalty, a price premium, and positive Equity.

ENERGY ENHANCES ONE-TO-ONE MARKETING

Just imagine how happy people would be if the only exchanges they had with a company were ones that legitimately engaged or interested them. Direct mail and marketing phone calls to people's homes would be welcome because they'd provide useful information or offer the chance to buy something desirable. Up-selling and cross-selling pitches delivered at the cash register wouldn't be a nuisance. Presale experiences and postsale follow ups would be entertaining, even exciting.

Any company pursuing Emotion Marketing should avoid messages and exchanges that needlessly take up consumers' time, slow them down, or are uninteresting. A company should instead strive to engage each customer on an individual basis, using interactions tailored specifically for him or her. By communicating one-to-one, businesses show they respect people's time, understand their unique needs, and care about meeting them. Burdening people with the wrong messages or time-consuming details pulls them away from participating in the rest of their lives.

This perfect level of one-to-one marketing is still a ways off but should nevertheless remain a goal. Emotion Marketing strategies, on the other

> *By communicating one-to-one, businesses show they respect people's time, understand their unique needs, and care about meeting them. Burdening people with the wrong messages or time-consuming details pulls them away from participating in the rest of their lives.*

hand, can bring results today by offering consumers time-saving enhancements—because every gesture that enhances Energy results in positive deposits to people's emotional bank accounts. Consumers are eager to make these deposits, too, because they yearn to give loyalty to a company in exchange for feeling valued and recognized.

And as studies have proven, consumers who provide loyalty also provide profits.

TO SUM IT UP

- Energy is made of time—and in today's society, people's time is being stretched in more directions than ever.
- By letting consumers focus their time on the important activities, events, and people in their lives—as opposed to transactional product details—companies make an emotional connection with them.
- Conserving people's energy also sends the message that a company values its customers. Wasting their time, on the other hand, says a company doesn't care.
- There are many ways to conserve time: making a product or service more accessible, easier, worthwhile, or personalized.
- Companies can use technology and information combined with security to empower customers with the ability to create even more time.
- Effectively managing people's Energy implies that all exchanges with the company are interesting and engaging to the customer. Not wasting a person's time enhances a one-to-one marketing strategy.

CHAPTER SIX

Product and Money— The Rational Side of the Value Star^SM

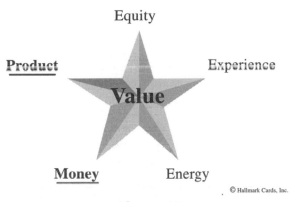

Figure 11

The power of emotion is indisputable. Marketers must nurture relation- ships with best customers to earn their loyalty. And loyalty, as many studies have proven, is the most powerful variable driving profits. So what will become of companies that focus attention solely on the Emo- tional Es—Equity, Experience, and Energy—neglecting the other two points of the Value Star^SM, Product and Money?

Even the most sophisticated Emotion Marketers recognize the importance of shoring up the *rational* components of their relationships with consumers. As strong as the Emotional Es are, even they can't overcome a poor value.

While emotional connections are what sway a person's purchase decisions, it's reliable, relevant product at a reasonable price that first gets a brand into the decision set. Put another way, consumers always expect solid Product and Money components. They are a basic requirement, the cost of entry into an industry. While Equity, Experience, and Energy help a company *win,* Product and Money are absolutely necessary for it to even *play* the game in the first place.

THE EVOLUTION OF CHOICE

Decades ago, when a family needed to buy something as simple as, say, new shoes for the coming school year, they likely drove to the local department store or specialty shoe retailer. Once there, the family had a few styles and manufacturers to choose from. Options were simple, and the purchase uncomplicated.

The idea of loyalty was equally simple. Whether satisfied or not, the family was likely to return to the same store the following year and purchase the same brand of shoe merely because they didn't have access to a wide range of choices. Until recently, repeat business may not have been based in loyalty at all, but on consumers' inability to have their needs satisfied anywhere else.

Years passed and, of course, the marketplace evolved so drastically that now this family's scenario seems almost quaint. Today, a family looking for shoes has many more department and shoe stores—at more malls—to choose from. Or they can browse mass merchandisers like Target and Kmart, catalogs like JCPenney and Speigel, and web sites like Payless.com and Bluefly.com.

Any retailer or manufacturer that doesn't satisfy customers by delivering a good-quality, relevant product at a fair price will force withdrawals from people's emotional bank accounts. If a customer is a first-time buyer, there's little or no trust (Equity) stashed away in reserve. A negative withdrawal in this case means a person will likely never give the brand another chance. There are simply too many other players out there competing fiercely for people's attention and dollars.

If a company is fortunate enough to have already established some emotional capital via successful interactions, a consumer dissatisfied for the first time may give the brand another try. The best-case scenario happens when a company establishes ways to find out about customers' experiences, both good and bad. Knowing a customer has been disappointed gives the marketer an important second chance to restore the person's trust. Hallmark has found that a sincere, timely apology showing genuine concern, followed by prompt action to fix the problem, leads to a marked increase in overall loyalty and feelings of trust.

> *People new to Emotion Marketing may be surprised to know that giving money or a gift to make up for a poor experience often backfires.*

People new to Emotion Marketing may be surprised to know that giving money or a gift to make up for a poor experience often backfires. In this case, customers suspect nobody at the company empathizes with their disappointment, and that the money or gift comes merely as a bribe. An extreme but very relevant example is a restaurant customer who gets food poisoning. A timely, sincere apology would be appreciated along with any reimbursements for medicine. Anything else—money, a gift, a certificate to visit the restaurant again—would be confusing if not insulting.

Brands that don't deliver on Product and Money won't get the chance to even *explore* the power of Equity, Experience, and Energy. Consumers will find other, often indistinguishable choices in the marketplace—and they'll probably do so quickly and easily. As strong as the Emotional Es are, they simply cannot overcome the disappointment a consumer feels when a company fails to follow through on the basics.

Saturn's Product Challenge

As successful as it has been strengthening relationships with a compelling overall Experience, Saturn faced a serious Product challenge several years ago. When the brand launched in 1990, Saturn positioned its identity as a maker of small cars. Its range was limited to three models—all compact—and while prices were perceived as very fair, they weren't the lowest. Nevertheless, Saturn offered a solid enough value proposition to place its cars squarely in target consumers' decision set.

The company didn't need to bury their competition with the very best vehicles at an unbelievable price, because it had a strong *emotional* strategy: Coupled with a solid Product/Money combination, Saturn staged a comfortable, no-pressure shopping experience and terrific postpurchase events, following up regularly with relationship-building touchpoints. The company's strategy helped Saturn build Equity, earn a decent price margin, and win the compact car game—for a while, at least.

Eventually, target customers' lives evolved, along with their automotive needs and incomes. Saturn models, however, failed to grow with them. The parent company, General Motors, likely hoped most drivers would migrate to other GM brands, trading up for Pontiac or Buick vehicles. But many never did. These people were accustomed to overwhelmingly positive emotional interactions, and didn't have enough trust accumulated in their bank accounts to consider other GM brands. So when people outgrew Saturn, they frequently checked out of GM altogether. No longer were the rational components of the Value Star[SM] relevant enough to overcome strong emotional bonds.

Recently, Saturn responded to their Product concerns, adding a midsized model to their car line. Time will reveal whether the company's Equity is strong enough—and customers' emotional bank accounts big enough—to win over people as effectively as it's done in the past.

ENHANCING THE RATIONAL COMPONENTS OF THE VALUE STAR^{SM}

Product and Money are not only required to *enter* an industry, but also to *stay* in it. And since the marketers' job is to get consumers to buy more from a company, they must regularly examine how much value the products deliver, never overlooking the rational points of the Value Star^{SM}. Fortunately, there are many ways to enhance these elements.

Improving Product

Add features. This is frequently the first strategy a company takes in improving its product or service. But a big downside awaits: the potential for competitors to fast-follow. The wisest companies will anticipate and prepare for competitive responses while developing their new product features—not after launching them.

The best barriers to prevent fast-following are the non-negotiable, structural kind. Can a company patent a feature, or even the product itself? Are there unique, creative elements that can be copyrighted or trademarked? Does the feature impact the manufacturing or delivery to such an extent that the lead time to duplicate it is insurmountable?

In the absence of these hard and fast barriers, there still may be alternatives to throwing a great idea into the marketplace and watching competitors grab it away. When barriers to entry aren't legally or structurally imposed, marketers shouldn't give up. They should get creative.

For example, a brand can position its new feature as a recognition gift or a premium for best customers. When the company eventually rolls out the feature to other consumers, there may be an extra shine to it—a benefit of delivering something as an exclusive offer, before calculatingly giving others access to it.

Another tactic would be to give the feature a creative name, since a company that introduces a solution to the world naturally gets to call it what it wants. A company could integrate the brand name into the feature name so the two are permanently linked. Think of Nike Air or Reebok Pump athletic shoes.

The company can then go to great lengths to *promote* it. What if marketers went beyond introducing a feature? What if they *celebrated* it, let the world know that their brand is the one to deliver innovation, solve problems, and delight its customers?

An overall goal for companies introducing an impressive new feature is to make sure they get credit for it. Even if competitors are able to duplicate this solution, they won't be able to hijack the emotional benefit earned by introducing it. The feature will be part of the bond between the innovating company and their customers. Consider that people probably can't recall which gas station originally offered a pay-at-the-pump option. But many *do* remember it was Ziploc who introduced the yellow-and-blue-make-green seal, and 3M who gave us Post-it notes.

Improve quality. Think of durable goods that last longer, smaller commodities that don't break apart, food that tastes better, or services that are more reliable. Quality can also be extended to packaging (making it extra durable or innovative) or to service (making it excellent or offering an extended warranty).

Improving quality has a few positive side effects, too. First, it relieves some of the pressure from a customer service department. With better product quality and fewer complaints, a company can redirect resources away from things like repairs, returns, and replacements, and invest them in the Emotional Es, the product itself, or the bottom line.

Second, more than any other product dimension, quality can have a profound impact on Equity. Reliably constructed products and impeccably delivered services result in a strong halo effect for a brand. Poor quality is a fast ticket to a negative brand reputation and stories of customer disappointment that may never go away.

Enhance design. The new Volkswagen Beetle is revolutionizing the automobile industry and reflecting a resurgence in style across industrial design. Automakers spent so long maximizing their vehicles' efficiency, minimizing wind resistance, and trying strenuously not to offend any consumers' taste, that cars began to all look strikingly similar, hatched from the same aerodynamic egg. The whimsical, nostalgic, and totally unexpected shape and feel of the Beetle wound up delighting drivers and reintroducing individuality to the auto industry. It gave Volkswagen a powerful platform to differentiate itself—and made vehicle designers some of the hottest, most-sought-after employees in the auto industry.

"[Quality] is no longer the determining factor for which brand to buy. That's why we are so turned on by the iMac and Beetle. Design is 'la différence.' In a world loaded with stuff that looks like all the other stuff and performs like all the other stuff, it is a way to stand out."

Tom Peters
Author and Management Consultant[32]

Why the reemphasis on design? Why are today's consumers buying designer hammers, neon-colored pagers, and Martha Stewart anything?

Over the years, as competition for consumers' wallets grew unrelenting, companies relied on homogenization and technology to relieve price pressure. Without realizing it, they were taking the soul out of product designs, leaving behind a bland, sterile marketplace. Essentially, businesses created a void in the marketplace, which translated into a big opportunity for innovators to stand out by simply appealing to the eye.

Macintosh, for instance, upped the ante for technology manufacturers everywhere by putting its iMac computers in fruit-colored casing. Electronic equipment of all kinds soon followed suit. Meanwhile, Crate and Barrel began selling a set of German-designed stainless steel bar tools with human and animal faces playfully integrated in their design. And mass merchandiser Target distinguished itself from the competition by hiring an upscale designer to retool such basics as toasters and teakettles. All these companies are winning on Product, and have earned the ability—at least temporarily—to charge a price premium for their surprising, eye-catching style.

Increase selection and availability.   Another way to win on Product is to make sure customers will always be able to have their needs filled without turning to a competitor. Not to be confused with an unfocused strategy of providing everything to everyone, increasing selection and availability means paying close attention to target customers, predicting their pur-chase behavior, and responding with a full range of products—consis-tently in stock—to satisfy them.

The major breakfast cereal makers, for instance, impact selection by developing wide product lines—ones that are big enough so a mom can find anything her family may have the taste for. Sweet, healthy, simple, even nostalgic choices are all covered. Several years ago, as families grew busier and set aside less time for meals, cereal makers responded with an entirely new category: breakfast bars. Portable, convenient snacks like this were necessary to keep target families from going to other brands or checking out of the cereal aisle altogether.

Blockbuster studied home entertainment customers and found that a significant percentage leave video stores empty-handed, unable to find the movie they came in for. Marketers teamed with their technology group to create a predictive model to forecast consumer demand. The program, which factors in variables like consumer demographics and past rental behavior, helps Blockbuster distribute an accurate quantity of new releases to each individual store. Ultimately, they guarantee a movie will be in stock when a customer wants it—a considerable competitive advantage.

Adding uniqueness or personalization.   On the opposite end of the spec-trum from increasing selection is developing a solution so unique that consumers will find it difficult to pass up, thinking they may never find it again. Often this strategy can include personalizing the product, limiting availability to make the item collectible, injecting a unique perspective or personality into it, or including a compelling story behind its creation.

J. C. Hall on Motivations for Success

from *When You Care Enough*, published by Hallmark Cards, Inc., 1979

If a man goes into business only with the idea of making a lot of money, chances are he won't. But if he puts service and quality first, the money will take care of itself. Producing a first-class product that is a real need is a much stronger motivation for success than getting rich.

If a man runs a hotel as well as Hernando Courtright ran the Beverly Hills Hotel, he'll make money. If he runs a magazine as well as DeWitt Wallace and Lila Acheson Wallace ran the *Reader's Digest*, he'll make money. If he runs a store as well as Marshall Field did, he'll make money. But more importantly, he'll make a real contribution to society.

Furniture and home decor manufacturers discovered this several years ago as an alternative to the mass-produced, overly clean look of some items. Companies began using distressed wood, flawed glass, and rough-cast metal to create one-of-a-kind character and charm. Instead of hiding the imperfections, companies drew attention to them, positioning them as special, enticing elements. Apparel manufacturers use distinctive patterns, faded material, and unexpected swatches to add variety not only *among* different clothing items, but often *within* a selection of the same item.

Improving Money

Historically, cost-based pricing had been the default method companies chose for pricing their products and services. Long before the market-place became so complex—back when choices were limited, competition was tame, and marketing hadn't evolved into the power it is today—it made sense for a manufacturer to let its finance people handle cost-making decisions. They considered how much money it required to make a product (materials, overhead, labor, distribution, etc.), then marked it up a certain percentage.

Companies gradually began adopting other philosophies, like setting prices based on consumers' perceived value, or strategically responding to competitors' pricing decisions. Whatever the process, marketers need to ensure that the Money component of the Value Star^{SM} is at least fair enough that it gets their brand into the playing field—and that they choose a pricing method that is right for their business. Here are some options to consider:

Promotions. Onetime or short-term discount offers can get consumers off the fence to try a brand, or potentially cross-sell new product to existing customers. Companies, however, should use price promotions carefully and strategically, for the wrong discount decisions can have negative effects. Relying on promotions too heavily during the customer acquisition stage could result in a company attracting a financially unappealing consumer—one who is extremely price sensitive and will likely disappear as soon as the discount does. An Emotion Marketer interested in building a long-term bond with customers will have difficulty doing so if they've set unrealistic Money expectations or trained consumers to wait for discounts.

> *Relying on promotions too heavily during the customer acquisition stage could result in a company attracting a financially unappealing consumer—one who is extremely price sensitive and will likely disappear as soon as the discount does.*

Marketers must also ensure that their price promotions aren't widely used by consumers ready to make the purchase regardless of price. And they must be cautious not to discount so frequently that people begin to question a brand's real worth. Doubts like this can erode trust and damage Equity.

When marketers have determined that a price promotion is a viable strategy, the program will be most successful if positioned in terms of the company/customer relationship. Marketers can communicate a promotion as a certificate of appreciation when cross-selling to existing customers. Or they can introduce products and services to new customers as an invitation to join a community. Both strategies will have positive benefits to loyalty and avoid some of the problems above.

Everyday low pricing. This has been an increasingly popular strategy in recent years as companies attempt to attract busy consumers. The inherent message that everyday low pricing delivers is that people don't have to spend time shopping around for the best deals. This Money strategy, though, comes with some of the same disadvantages as promotions—like the tendency to attract customers intolerant of price increases.

Everyday low pricing is now approaching standard protocol for many retail outlets and requires constant, unrelenting attention to efficiency. A low-price company will only succeed if it's also the low-cost producer.

Breadth of prices. Much like using a wide selection of merchandise to improve consumer Product perception, a company can offer a range of *prices* to satisfy all its consumers' Money needs.

Procter & Gamble, for instance, knows that not all consumers are willing to pay a premium for their high-Equity detergent Tide. So they supplement the brand with less expensive options like Cheer and Era. Fine restaurants are wise to offer two or three less expensive entrées on their menus, since guests usually walk into a restaurant without a precise idea of how much the meals will cost. Having many different entrée prices ensures diners of finding something within their expected price range so they won't have to leave in search of a more moderately priced restaurant.

Consumer control

"Consumers are agnostic."

Jan Murley

Hallmark Group Vice President of Marketing

The Internet has given people access to a staggering amount of information. Of all this new data, they seem most interested in web sites that help research prices and find great values. The information explosion has armed consumers, making them wary of the prices they pay both online and off. Whether browsing a traditional retail store, catalog, or web site, shoppers know better bargains may be right around the corner—or just a couple clicks away.

Consumers feel in control. And they like it. They can see the man behind the curtain, so to speak, and have raised their expectations about how companies must follow through on their Money position.

Marketers may look at this shift in power and feel the temptation to respond by matching the lowest price available. A better tactic in the long run, however, may be to *appeal* to the consumers' sense of control. Satisfying the Money component doesn't automatically imply cutting prices and sacrificing margins—it may mean thinking creatively and giving consumers better pricing devices.

For instance, companies providing big-ticket items or services can communicate the kind of up-front, fair, no-haggle pricing that Saturn made famous. The automaker was definitely out front in the Money game, making shoppers feel they were in command. Once, car negotiations were uncomfortable, almost scripted discussions among the buyer, salesperson, and an unseen member of management. But Saturn removed all the mystery embedded in pricing negotiations, taking Money decisions from the backroom and putting them squarely in the customers' control. Think of all the emotional bank account withdrawals that Saturn avoided by protecting shoppers from an experience they've always distrusted.

Online auction sites like eBay and agents like Priceline.com put consumers in command by letting them determine the price they're willing to pay. And grocery chains clearly display prices of store-branded products next to name brands, often highlighting the difference. "The choice is yours," the store is communicating. "And here's precisely how much that decision will cost you."

Some of the most emotionally unappealing Money experiences today happen in the airline industry. Consumers who speak with reservations agents hear firsthand how wildly prices fluctuate based on factors largely irrelevant to the flier. Once on the airplane, customers are left wondering if they paid significantly higher than the person in the next seat, despite the fact that the Product is exactly the same. Consumers recognize they are not the ones in control in this relationship. Skepticism festers and, in response, online booking and pricing alternatives pop up, offering to shift control back to the customer.

Marketers must perpetually ask themselves not only if they can set different prices, but if they can *position* those prices differently—not unlike the examples above. What if a company can actually find out precisely how much each consumer is willing to pay, then deliver goods accordingly? Or if it gave shoppers "inside information" on its pricing, automatically and constantly keeping consumers up-to-date on impending reductions or increases? Or if it advised consumers that switching to different products or services could save them money?

As with Product, marketers need to think creatively as they reevaluate and improve their Money positions.

More important, they need to think like their consumers.

THE POWER OF EMOTION REVISITED

In today's cluttered marketplace, with seemingly unlimited choices, winning on Product and Money is a remarkable accomplishment. A company that outshines competitors on these rational points of the Value Star^{SM}

should feel pretty good about its work—but shouldn't spend too long congratulating itself, because the Product and Money race never really ends. Advantages are difficult or impossible to sustain.

Money is the easiest marketing tool for a competitor to replicate. Pricing decisions are, after all, public knowledge, and a business can't protect them legally or build fences around them. Once they've lowered the price, marketers abdicate control to competitors that can decide to match or beat it. And in a commodity market, they'll have no choice *but* to match or beat it. There's nothing differentiable about a price that a "Sale" sign or pricing gun can't change immediately.

> *Money is the easiest marketing tool for a competitor to replicate. There's nothing differentiable about a price that a "Sale" sign or pricing gun can't change immediately.*

Leading an industry in a price war comes at a significant cost. Margins suffer, revenues are driven down, and resources are reallocated away from other sources like innovation, quality, or service. Management is under constant pressure to reengineer, cut back, and squeeze bottom-line dollars from their budgets. That pressure naturally cascades down to the rest of the organization.

Trying to win on Product is safer—but not by much. Despite some of the protective measures, competitors can get wily when it comes to duplicating features or imitating designs. Even when Product is difficult to replicate, it may instead be subject to society's constantly evolving tastes and needs. How long before a breakthrough feature becomes irrelevant? Or the whole product or service itself? In the new economy, the time may be discouragingly short.

This is especially valid with technological products and services. Insiders have said a year in the real world is equivalent to three months in the technology industry. Standard business planning is becoming more challenging as companies reinvent business models and value propositions at a quickening pace.

Take electronic postage providers like E-stamps and Stamps.com. When they launched a few years ago, their value proposition—letting companies and consumers avoid trips to the post office by digitally printing postage directly onto envelopes—looked compelling enough to set stock prices flourishing. Now, though, today's roiling business environment threatens these companies' viability. Direct mail houses want a live stamp on their mail to increase open rates. More businesses are relying on e-mail to deliver documents and messages. And bills are increasingly being sent and paid via electronic banking and financial web sites. Like online stamp providers, many companies—even entire industries—face a double threat: Not only can competitors put them underwater, but society could just as easily render them irrelevant as it evolves.

For these reasons and more, businesses must approach Product and Money differently than they do Equity, Experience, and Energy. Not all points on the Value Star^{SM} are created equal.

While a solid, rational value is a necessary cost to enter a marketplace, a brand cannot win on Product and Money over the long run. Competitors will grab most rational advantages and try to make them their own. A brand must position itself ahead of the marketplace by reinforcing its position using Equity, Experience, and Energy— because these advantages can't be commoditized or copied. In addition, the Emotional Es aren't restricted to product categories. Strong emotional bonds with consumers give companies the permission to successfully enter—even prosper in—other industries.

> *The emotional realm is where relationships are established and loyalty thrives. This is where the rest of the marketplace will have a hard time following. This is where the game is won.*

The emotional realm is where relationships are established and loyalty thrives. This is where the rest of the marketplace will have a hard time following. *This is where the game is won.*

Think of each point on the Value Star^{SM} having a range of levels: from positive to neutral to negative. (See Figure 12.) A company must strategically position its brand in the range of all five dimensions. Then it needs to determine how to communicate to consumers so their perceptions overlap with brand identity.

Hallmark, as we've seen, has decided to focus on Product and Equity. The company followed up with initiatives like the *12 Attributes of Compelling Product* to enhance the Product dimension, and *Hallmark Hall of Fame* movies to strengthen Equity.

Starbucks' strategy is to lead with Product and Experience. Though price was an issue at first with consumers who had never paid a couple dollars for a cup of coffee, competitors didn't respond with stronger Money positions, and people's price expectations evolved along with the brand's Equity.

The company is a Product innovator because it gives large numbers of coffee drinkers access to gourmet coffees imported from around the world. While their beverages and prices earn Starbucks a spot in consumers' decision sets, the company relies on Experience to dominate and be a catalyst for industry growth. Most of its customers, especially early on, were busy city dwellers in cluttered urban environments. They were drawn to Starbucks because the stores gave them a setting—and permission—to pause and relax. Customers were *satisfied* by the Product, but

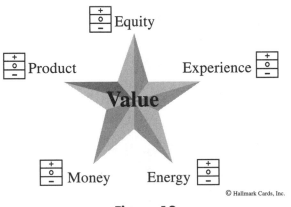

© Hallmark Cards, Inc.

Figure 12

J. C. Hall on "The Very Best"

from *When You Care Enough,* published by Hallmark Cards, Inc., 1979

For many years we tried to come up with a slogan that would do the best job advertising Hallmark cards. We started with "Hallmark Cards Say What You Want to Say, the Way You Want to Say It"—which was quite a mouthful. On the Tony Wons program we used, "Look for the Hallmark and Crown on the Back of the Card." But these were entirely geared to promoting a brand name without emphasizing quality.

Ed Goodman, who was responsible for advertising and sales, put together a number of slogans that were more like a commercial than a single message. His original draft, on a three-by-five-inch card, appeared as follows:

Three little words that mean so much—a Hallmark Card
   They tell your friends you cared enough
to send the very best
   They best reflect your perfect taste . . .
your thoughtfulness.
So . . . Before you buy—Look on the back for those three identifying words . . . A HALLMARK CARD

We began picking out bits and pieces. For several years we used "Hallmark Cards Best Reflect Your Perfect Taste, Your Thoughtfulness." Ed wanted to emphasize caring as the key to the slogan. And there it was—buried in the various phrases we had been using. In 1944 we adapted it to read: "When You Care Enough to Send the Very Best."

While we thought we had only established a good advertising slogan, we soon found out we had made a business commitment as well. The slogan constantly put pressure on us to make Hallmark cards "the very best." We have thrown away many millions of cards that did not justify that commitment. I somehow feel that without the slogan our products would not have been as good. And there is no question that the slogan had a favorable effect on the buying public.

A strong emotional component will transcend consumers' rational thoughts and appeal to their hearts. And the heart, after all, is where purchase decisions are made and bonds between company and consumer are established.

they *sought out* the Experience: a chance to slow the world down and take it in, one cup at a time. This is a very powerful emotional platform, and as Starbucks has rapidly expanded, they've never strayed far from it.

Brands are unable to lead in all five Value Star[SM] categories because of scarce resources: businesses can only spend so much money, and consumers can only absorb a limited amount of media messages in today's crowded, noisy environment. Conclusion? Marketers cannot win on all five Value Star[SM] points. They must instead decide carefully where they want their brand to excel, and which dimensions they are willing to deemphasize.

Hallmark has found that to win, brands must accomplish two goals. One, they must have no disadvantages. No points of the Value Star[SM] should be in the negative zone. Consumers are simply not loyal enough to tolerate a strong negative component when they can jump to other options instead. If Equity is too weak, consumers won't believe the company's messages about, say, a positive Money position. Similarly, no Product, regardless of its features or benefits, will succeed if it requires too much Energy to acquire or consume.

Hallmark's *12 Attributes of Compelling Product*

Defining "emotion" is tougher than it sounds. The dictionary definition does nothing to tell you how to turn a card into a keepsake or write a letter that gives the recipient goose bumps. There are, however, some evocative elements that give a product personality or turn a service into a treat.

Some of those elements are listed below. As part of a product leadership initiative, a 20-person Hallmark team examined nearly 300 different consumer products and generated a list of their most compelling characteristics. Hallmark's creative staff now assesses new products—from greeting cards to home decor—against these *12 Attributes of Compelling Product.* Other companies might alter the list to be more relevant to their industries—for example, adding *safety* for automobiles, or *convenience* for credit cards.

1. *Worth.* The product provides benefits that outweigh its cost.
2. *Emotional Intent.* The product has an emotional purpose, and all the elements work together to serve it.
3. *Originality.* Lends the excitement of something never before seen: a new technique, idea, or point of view; a unique personality.
4. *Authenticity & Passion.* The product resonates with real experience and/or the convictions of its creator.
5. *Craftsmanship & Artistry.* Emotional effects are heightened by flawless craft and masterful use of artistic devices (color, scale, perspective, rhythm, repetition).
6. *Storytelling.* Creates emotion through virtual experience; brings universal experiences and truths to life with vivid detail.

7. *Memories.* The product taps into past experiences, where our deepest reservoirs of emotion lie, or helps create new memories.
8. *Relevance.* Answers the question: What does this have to do with me?
9. *Timeliness/Timelessness.* The product's benefits match a person's needs at a particular time or address the deepest human needs that never change.
10. *Sensory/Experiential.* Color, scent, motion, and other interactive effects engage participation and create emotion.
11. *Range.* Variety in emotional tone and intensity, both within and between product lines, makes them more interesting.
12. *Critical Mass.* Intentional groupings of product that build greater emotional impact than individual products could do alone.

Second, brands must dominate in at least two dimensions—and at least one of those must be an Emotional E. A strong emotional component will transcend consumers' rational thoughts and appeal to their hearts. And the heart, after all, is where purchase decisions are made and bonds between company and consumer are established.

Jif has been an incredibly strong brand of peanut butter for decades. Jif followed Emotion Marketing strategies long before the principles were widely articulated. Back in the 1950s and 1960s, before women entered the workforce in large numbers, an unwritten rule existed in society saying the best mothers served their kids hot lunches. Jif faced two challenges—standing out among other brands, and overcoming strong standards about how people should and should not use its product.

The brand had already established strong rational positions (especially among the ultimate consumer, children, who have always loved the Product) to compete against other peanut butter makers. So Jif relied on emotion to drive its communications with consumers. "Choosy mothers choose Jif" let women feel good about serving their families a cold lunch. A peanut butter sandwich became not just an acceptable but a preferred meal. The best mothers who cared most about their families chose to buy Jif. While a good product at a reasonable price got the brand into target customers' decision set, Equity cemented the bond and made the brand take off.

At first glance it may appear like Wal-Mart defies the Value Star^{SM} rules by competing on Money. The retailer consistently articulates to consumers that it's the low-price leader, and in the future will continue to roll back prices. But if Money is the easiest marketing component to duplicate, and causes margins to spiral downward, how is it that Wal-Mart has thrived?

While price is surely a powerful message the company delivers, it actually wins on more subtle strategies. All of which are emotional. Wal-Mart has identified a vivid brand identity. It's all about small-town values, friendliness, and a pro-American presence. This personality is the consumers' image of the brand as well, meaning that their message has been communicated and perceived accurately. Wal-Mart has developed a bond with customers based on trust—and where there's trust, there's Equity.

The company complements its Equity with other emotional messages, too. Store greeters and clean, organized environments differentiate the Wal-Mart shopping experience from many other retailers. And consumers perceive the store is strong on Energy as well, offering a one-stop shopping Experience where everything they need will be available.

Is it any wonder that Wal-Mart consistently beats its closest competitors? Or that it was one of the factors leading another mass retailer, Venture, to close its doors? Or that it is now on deck to become, literally, the biggest company in the world? To their target consumers the company has no negative levels in any Value Star^{SM} dimensions. It's at least solid or strong on the rational points, Product and Money, drawing people into the stores. And its emotional messages have kept people coming back.

Managing your value proposition using the Value Star^{SM} truly is the key to Emotion Marketing. It's the way brands build loyalty in an age when loyalty is difficult to find. It's the difference between relevant, durable brands like Disney, Coca-Cola, Nike, and Harley-Davidson versus the also-rans. It's the reason these names have staked their claim not only in consumer purchase behavior, but in our culture as well.

TO SUM IT UP

- In today's new economy, consumers have an enormous array of choices to meet their needs. If a company fails to offer a solid product value, consumers will have an easy time defecting to a competitor.
- Product and Money, the rational points of the Value Star^{SM}, are the cost of entry into a competitive market. A brand will win based on the Emotional Es, but satisfying the rational side is necessary to get into consumers' decision sets in the first place.
- Choosing to lead solely on Product and Money is not a sound strategy—they're the easiest marketing tools for a competitor to replicate, and do not represent a sustainable, competitive advantage.
- Since companies have limited resources to deliver messages, and consumers have limited time to hear them, a brand can't win on all five points of the Value Star^{SM}. It should decide strategically which dimensions it will lead with and which it will deliberately not emphasize.
- To win in the marketplace, a company has to meet two objectives:
  1. lead on at least two of the five Value Star^{SM} dimensions, including one or more from the emotional side—this will help build a competitive asset that other brands cannot easily copy.
  2. be at least neutral on the other dimensions to ensure a brand remains in consumers' decision sets.

PART THREE

How to Put Emotion Marketing to Work

CHAPTER SEVEN

Building Customer Relationships That Last

The Value Star^{SM} works at three different levels.

First, it can serve as a framework for evaluating a brand's overall value proposition compared to the competition. A product manufacturer might try to find out whether customer perceptions match up with the company's identity. A retail chain might rethink its shopping environment. A web site might cut a few clicks from the order process.

But savvy marketers don't stop with an overview. The second application of the Value Star^{SM} is as a means of analyzing value as defined by specific consumer segments. Distribution channels might be affected by customer preference for a rich shopping experience or a minimum expenditure of energy. Different product offerings could be developed for brand- and price-conscious customers.

Hallmark research identified a segment of customers who highly valued the Hallmark brand and enjoyed the shopping experience of card shops. Equity and Experience were key value drivers for this group, and Hallmark's existing value proposition was on target.

But another segment was far more concerned with time constraints. They appreciated the Hallmark brand and product quality—but often couldn't make the special trip to a Hallmark card shop. In Value Star[SM] terms, Energy was the key value driver for this group; to save time, they preferred to buy greeting cards in stores they already frequented, like supermarkets and general merchandise stores. Hallmark launched Expressions from Hallmark, and distributed it to mass channel retailers committed to providing quality brand name products. This allowed the time-starved consumer segment to save time while still meeting its need for branded, quality products.

> *Emotion Marketing is about more than predicting and meeting needs: The ultimate goal is to develop an enduring connection with each customer.*

Finally, the Value Star[SM] can assess an individual's motivations and help custom-tailor a product or service to personal preference. Internet companies that offer suggestions based on stated preferences and past purchases take full advantage of new technology to conserve Energy—one customer at a time.

Emotion Marketing is about more than predicting and meeting needs: The ultimate goal is to develop an enduring connection with each customer. And to do that, *an organization must understand that building relationships is a process, not an event—and its leadership must be willing to make a long-term investment in loyalty.*

GETTING TO KNOW THE CUSTOMER

Hallmark's Gold Crown Card loyalty program rang up $1.5 billion in sales in 1999. The program's success was due in large part to understanding its active members—over 12 million of them—and addressing their needs. Quarterly member mailings typically include a statement of points accumulated in the loyalty program, a coupon for dollars off merchandise based on the point level, and a brochure featuring greeting cards, gift-related products, and tips for celebrating occasions and recognizing relationships.

The Gold Crown Program has divided its database into seven distinct segments; two of them, for example, are "card enthusiasts" and "ornament enthusiasts." Elements of each mailing are customized to be relevant to each segment *and* cost-effective for Hallmark. Customers who show less potential for purchases receive fewer mailings and/or less-expensive packages, like postcards instead of multipiece letters.

Whether through the personal contact possible with smaller companies or the intense formal research required of large organizations, knowing customers and understanding their unique needs are critical to enhancing value. And for Emotion Marketing, segmentation by transaction or purchase behavior is only the first step.

To be actionable, each segment a company defines must also take into account personal attributes—life stage, for example. A retail bank might focus offers to young single customers on IRAs, direct deposits, and car loans. When these customers marry, mortgages become a concern. Parents with children at home are interested in college funds and life insurance annuities. Empty nesters can be targeted with information about investments and estate planning.

Obviously, there are many additional segments based on demographic, lifestyle, and attitudinal characteristics—along with transactional behavior.

THE EMOTIONAL EKG: LOYALTY ACROSS THE CUSTOMER LIFE CYCLE

Over each segment, companies then lay the template of the customer life cycle. Just as personal relationships develop over time, customers relate to businesses differently at different points: the introductory steps of *Acquisition,* the getting-to-know-each-other *Assimilation* phase, ongoing *Cultivation* efforts, and the sometimes difficult *Reactivation* stage. (See Figure 13.)

And just as people's emotional needs change through the course of relationships with family and friends, consumers' emotional connections with businesses evolve.

Hallmark Loyalty Marketing Group developed the Emotional EKG to help companies monitor and anticipate how emotionally connected customers feel at different points during the behavior-oriented customer life cycle. Organizations can use the Emotional EKG as guidance for every aspect of their contacts with customers—from determining offers, to the content and tone of the message, to the frequency and cost of mailings.

Acquisition

The Acquisition stage spans the time from customers' initial awareness of a product or service to a trial purchase. During this stage, companies must break through the clutter to establish their brand identity and attract potential customers.

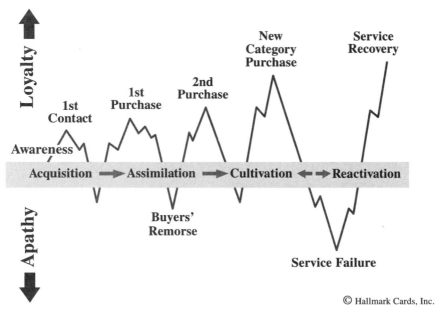

© Hallmark Cards, Inc.

Figure 13

The first challenge is targeting the right consumers. Statistical models can be built based on current high value customers and applied to the prospect pool to improve the quality of the prospect list and target customers likely to be loyal.

Challenge number two is making the right impression. Focusing on the relationship process, not merely on the transaction, is critical. This is the chance to set the stage for a lasting, mutually beneficial relationship. It's also an opportunity to begin building trust and setting customer expectations—unrealistic expectations established during Acquisition result in disappointment and dissatisfaction in the future.

Finally, it's important to avoid excessive use of incentives to acquire new customers. Discounts, gifts, and "bribes" tend to attract deal-oriented consumers who will switch providers once a better incentive comes along. Research shows excessive incentives also upset existing customers, who feel their loyalty is disregarded as best offers are given to new customers.

Assimilation

Stage two, Assimilation, is a critical and often misunderstood phase in the relationship-building process. This is the proverbial fork in the road. Based on the initial experience with the product/service provider, a customer will either progress to a strong sense of attachment or regress to apathy. At this stage in the relationship trust is fragile and can be easily broken; conversely, positive experiences early on will reinforce trust and encourage repeat usage.

Companies must immediately acknowledge and directly address potential buyers' remorse. *Emotion Marketing means welcoming customers, reinforcing their purchase decisions, and creating an exceptionally strong sense that they are important, valued, and cared about.*

Assimilation is also the time for customers to test the relationship, both consciously and subconsciously. Is a company willing to flex and evolve to meet various needs? Are emotional benefits present—not just rational ones? What incentive is there to purchase a second time?

The Power of One Loyal Customer

The passing of her husband at Christmastime propelled Clara Scroggins on a new course in life. She had always decorated several trees in her home with antique ornaments—but that year, in memory of her husband and the relationship they shared, Clara purchased a special sterling silver cross. It was the first in what would become a collection of crosses from around the world—and the beginning of her passion for collecting. When Hallmark began making Keepsake Ornaments, Clara jumped in with both feet. She explained, "I saw it: [ornament collecting] as something that helps to commemorate time and events."

Because she wanted to collect entire series of ornaments, Clara got in touch with Hallmark to find out which ones she'd missed. Her quest for information led her to write *Hallmark Keepsake Ornaments—A Collector's Guide;* 25 years later, the book is in its seventh edition.

She started the first local collector's club in Houston and convinced Hallmark to charter the Hallmark's Keepsake Ornaments Collector's Club. The club, now 200,000 members strong, appeals to members on several levels—not only do they receive special communications, members-only offers, and exclusive ornaments, but the deeper human need for belonging is also met, with local chapters, invitations to club events, personalized membership cards, and an online discussion board.

Hallmark and the club members aren't the only ones to benefit from Clara's efforts. She also helped develop an annual fund-raiser in Florida called the "Flamingo Fling" that attracts 600 to 1000 collectors from across the country. This year the weekend event raised $38,000 for Southeast Guide Dogs, a nonprofit group that trains guide dogs for the blind.

> Ultimately, Clara's work is about much more than just collecting Hallmark Keepsake ornaments. Over the years, she says, the clubs and her passion for ornaments have brought her "many, many, many, friendships."

Research shows that a customer who has purchased a second time is twice as likely to buy again than a one-time buyer. *With each purchase, customers indicate their willingness to move further into a loyal relationship. Smart companies will meet them more than halfway.*

Cultivation

After the second or third purchase, the Cultivation stage begins, and with it come opportunities to cement lifelong bonds.

Management consultants and futurists Don Peppers and Martha Rogers, Ph.D., talk about the relationship growing between a customer and business at this stage: "A Learning Relationship between a customer and an enterprise gets smarter and smarter with every individual interaction, defining in ever more detail the customer's own individual needs and tastes. A Learning Relationship ensures that it is always in the customer's self-interest to remain with the firm that has developed the relationship to begin with."[33]

Peppers and Rogers point out that this doesn't *have* to involve an emotional attachment. But Emotion Marketing adds caring to convenience—and as studies have shown, offering more than mere satisfaction significantly increases the chances a customer will remain loyal.

Emotion Marketing also allows clearer differentiation from competition—and the Learning Relationship arms a company with knowledge competitors don't have, allowing even more custom-tailored service. The emotional energy the customer invests in the learning process creates another reason to stay loyal.

During the Cultivation stage, companies also should:

Refine segmentation strategies. Continually evaluate and refine segmentation strategies as more information is gained about customers, aiming to become more relevant to each individual.

Capture lifetime value of profitable customer relationships. Track past purchase behavior and predict future transactions against acquisition and ongoing marketing costs to determine lifetime value. To help project potential future growth and understand customers' other choices, determine share of wallet—the amount of money customers are spending with the company and in the total category.

> *A sure sign of success in the Cultivation stage is the transformation of customers into apostles, eager to spread a company's message to the marketplace.*

Take advantage of cross-selling opportunities. Loyal customers are more receptive to cross-sell offers. And experience shows that individuals who purchase multiple products or services are more likely to remain loyal.

Request referrals. When customers become an organization's best salespeople, the company has created the most powerful marketing tool that exists. Referrals represent personal endorsements, proving the customers' loyalty and providing a compelling base of acquisition prospects.

A sure sign of success in the Cultivation stage is the transformation of customers into apostles, eager to spread a company's message to the marketplace.

Reactivation

Finally, there is the Reactivation stage. Despite its best efforts, every company risks losing customers because of service failures, changing consumer needs, and emerging competition. Reactivation actually involves two different approaches: Intervention and Win Back.

Intervention means identifying customers who have defected psychologically and renewing their investment in the relationship:

- Using attrition modeling, companies can identify likely defectors before they leave and take appropriate action based on potential reasons for attrition. For example, a credit card company might offer a lower interest rate. Or a retailer might offer exclusive services like free shipping, a private shopping night, special in-store seminars, or free gift wrap.
- In the case of a service failure, recovery efforts might include any approach from an apology to a gift to full compensation.

Win Back is about keeping the door open for lost customers to come back, or offering compelling, individually relevant reasons to try the company again. The key here is to understand why customers defect and to take steps to avoid repeating the same mistakes—by conducting exit interviews with dissatisfied customers, for example.

Again—as in people's personal lives—one bad experience doesn't necessarily mean the end of the business relationship. Rather, it can be an opportunity to respond quickly and win back a customer by admitting the error and fixing the problem. Communication remains key in this stage, since 55 percent of customers only complain "sometimes" when they're not satisfied, and eight percent never complain.[34] *Studies show customers who receive prompt and satisfactory resolu-*

> *The Emotional EKG reflects the fact that loyalty increases over time. Unfortunately, though, many companies spend the most money in the Acquisition stage—and invest much more in efforts to attract new customers than it would cost to retain their current ones.*

tions to problems—once again, indicating a company cares about them—will likely become even more loyal than before.

One more thing: It's all right to allow some customers to fall away. Experience shows most companies attract a group of customers that are unprofitable or require a disproportionate amount of resources to service. Divesting from this segment will actually improve the bottom line and free up resources to put toward profitable customers. The secret is knowing which ones to invest in keeping and which to let go.

The Emotional EKG reflects the fact that loyalty increases over time, reaching its highest level during *Cultivation*—or even *Reactivation*. Unfortunately, though, many companies spend the most money in the *Acquisition* stage—and invest much more in efforts to attract new customers than it would cost to retain their current ones. And ironically, many marketers spend their money acquiring the *wrong* customers. Offering financial incentives to switch telephone services or low introductory interest rates on a credit card draws the kind of customer who'll turn right around and switch again when the next offer comes along.

Often, this issue is exacerbated by organizational structure. Many companies organize their marketing function into separate acquisition and retention departments and fail to align their objectives. The result is often an acquisition department solely concerned about *quantity* of acquisition, not *quality*—it employs incentives to acquire new customers, regardless of their potential for long-term loyalty. The retention group then struggles to build loyalty among customers who may or may not fit the target customer profile.

Research shows these marketing tactics are causing existing customers to be less loyal at alarming rates.[35]

REQUIREMENTS OF LONG-TERM RELATIONSHIPS

To take full advantage of the insights provided in the Emotional EKG, companies must commit to the day-to-day requirements of building successful relationships. The elements are the same as those that exist between friends and family members:

Mutual benefit. Stephen Covey talks about "win-win" situations, where "one person's success is not achieved at the expense or exclusion of the success of others." Without a willingness to work for common good, a relationship can't grow. And without a clear benefit for either party, the relationship is destined to fail.

Commitment. The participants recognize the benefit and value of the relationship and are dedicated to making it work. The level of commitment must also progress over time, with a higher level of responsibility and interaction as the relationship develops.

Authenticity. Hidden agendas and disingenuousness inevitably are revealed; relationships require openness and sincerity on both sides. Customers are savvier than ever. If expressions of caring aren't sincere, customers will catch on and relationships will regress. Appreciation expressed genuinely will be noticed and will accelerate the evolution of the relationship.

Communication. Both parties must feel free to express themselves and know they'll be heard and understood.

By letting customers know how a company can provide something they value, consistently reinforcing its commitment to their needs, by speaking openly and honestly, and listening and responding to feedback, an organization indicates its willingness to earn customer loyalty.

This implies that companies must be willing to listen to customers and act upon their input. Emotional value is often exchanged through communication—whether it's a face-to-face meeting, e-mails between a customer and a service rep, or a birthday card sent to the customer. Without a healthy flow of communication, a Learning Relationship is impossible and the relationship will stagnate.

At every stage of a business relationship, well-thought-out *communication* helps the organization convey the other three factors to customers. By letting them know how a company can provide something they value, by consistently reinforcing its commitment to even their unspoken needs, by speaking openly and honestly, and by listening carefully and responding to feedback, an organization indicates its willingness to earn customer loyalty.

To quote Peppers and Rogers once more: "With each interaction—each time the firm and the customer reengage in their relationship—the company is able to fit its product or service a little more closely to the needs of *that* customer. In effect, the relationship is getting smarter and smarter, becoming better and better at satisfying that particular customer's need."

TO SUM IT UP

- Relationships are the soil in which emotional connections take root and grow. The relationship between a company and its customers provides the opportunity for a meaningful exchange of value.
- The Value Star^{SM} functions on three levels:
  1. To evaluate a brand's overall value proposition compared to the competition.
  2. To analyze value as perceived by different customer segments.

3. To help tailor products and services to individual preferences.

- Database segmentation by transaction or purchase behavior is only the first step—truly understanding value means taking into account life stage, demographics, and attitudinal characteristics.

- The Emotional EKG predicts how emotionally connected customers feel at different points on behavior-oriented customer life cycle and can guide customer contacts—including offers, the content and tone of the message, and the frequency of mailings. The four life cycle stages are: Acquisition, Assimilation, Cultivation, and Reactivation.

- Companies must commit to the day-to-day requirements of building successful relationships, including:

  1. Mutual benefit to both parties involved.
  2. Commitment and dedication to making the relationship work over time.
  3. Authenticity, openess, and genuine expressions of caring.
  4. Communication to help convey the other three elements.

CHAPTER EIGHT

Emotion in Marketing Communications

Mutual benefit, commitment, authenticity, and communication are essential elements of every relationship. In a business relationship, communication takes on added importance as the primary means of demonstrating the other three factors.

It's a fairly simple matter to add an emotional element to many kinds of communications it's already been mentioned that making emotional appeals is a common advertising practice. But a true Emotion Marketing strategy calls for going beyond an immediate response to appeal to deeper human needs—spiritual and personal motives like acceptance, self-esteem, self-image. Similarly, Emotion Marketing requires going beyond mass messages to relevant, customized communications.

Hallmark's research and experience, as well as the results of programs in a wide variety of industries, have made it clear that the drivers of Emotion Marketing transcend media.

Whether they're delivered through the mail, across the Internet, over the phone, or in person, effective Emotion Marketing communications are:

- personal and relevant
- relationship-focused
- unique and differentiated
- intended to create an emotional connection

One more point: Emotion Marketing also makes an important distinction between communications meant to drive transactions and those meant to build the customer relationship. Alternating between transactional exchanges, informational exchanges, and emotional exchanges is one of the keys to a successful communications plan. Balancing the types of communication allows an organization to generate short-term results while fostering long-term loyalty.

COMMUNICATION STRATEGY

Effective Emotion Marketing communications include all the elements of successful direct marketing. But beyond considerations such as targeting the right audience, making a compelling offer, developing strong creative solutions, and monitoring cost-effectiveness, there are five elements that are especially important to consider when determining an emotion-driven contact strategy. They are:

- Relevance
- Timing
- Sender/Recipient Relationship
- Frequency
- Perceived Value

Relevance

Simply put, a message must have meaning to the recipient to make an emotional connection. Relevance means sending the right message to the right person.

J. C. Hall *on* Understanding the Customer

from *When You Care Enough*, published by Hallmark Cards, Inc., 1979

Hallmark founder J. C. Hall used to say, "Each decision we make should best serve the needs and desires of the American public." He was constantly thinking of ways Hallmark could be more loyal to the people who sold and used its products.

Hall often said that regardless of the medium, "People will always have a need to communicate and Hallmark will offer the best possible way to do that." In the early 1900s he began the Hallmark tradition of the "research trip" by traveling 4000 miles through seven states, calling on 500 retailers, and talking to 1500 people about sentiments, paper, poetry, selling, drawers of cards, and anything else that influenced customers and retailers to buy and sell cards.

As a result of his trip, his company built new retail display fixtures and created a stock control system to enable retailers to keep tabs on inventory, reorder automatically, and rotate new items in for old. Creative staffs were charged with updating greeting card artwork and sentiments, and the paper stock was improved to withstand addressing and mailing.

J. C. Hall understood the importance of strong relationships with customers on every level: "After all," he said, "they are the people who pay the bills." He remained adamant that "the success or failure of Hallmark Cards, and the degree of either, is determined by how well it serves the queen, the buying public; and the king, the stores that retail Hallmark Cards."

An apartment dweller probably doesn't care about discounts on lawn mowers. Another offer for a credit card with a $2000 spending limit will only irritate the occupant with a lousy credit rating. "Thanks for being a great customer" means nothing to someone who hasn't made a purchase in recent memory.

When an organization has moved beyond target marketing to individualized, one-to-one marketing, it can deliver a relevant message that makes perfect sense as part of a customer's unique value proposition. When developing a piece, marketers should ask themselves: "Will the recipient understand the reason for getting this?" and "Is it meaningful and of interest to the recipient?"

Relevant communication makes a recipient feel known and valued. Pieces that are obviously part of a mass mailing to a random database just prove that a company doesn't know or care about potential, existing, or former customers.

> *Balancing communications meant to drive transactions and those meant to build the customer relationship. It allows an organization to generate short-term results while fostering long-term loyalty.*

Timing

Timing is a logical extension of relevance. Ideally, the right message gets to the right person at the right time—as determined by the calendar or the customer life cycle. *Sometimes communications might be expected—at other times surprising. But good timing means they're never unwelcome.*

Calendar-driven messages are obvious: A birthday greeting makes more sense if it arrives near the actual birthday. A "20 percent off all merchandise—all month" will be more appreciated if it's received on the first than the 25th. And an exclusive back-to-school offer should be received *before* the school term actually starts.

Timing contacts based on the Emotional EKG can all but guarantee maximizing the emotional high points in a customer's relationship with the company while minimizing negative experiences. At every stage there are opportunities for nonreciprocal, purely emotion-driven messages, well-targeted incentives for purchase behavior, and other contacts that assure customers that the company is looking out for their interests. Touchpoints to consider:

> *Relevant communication makes a recipient feel known and valued.*

Acquisition
>   High-impact lead generation contacts
>   Introductory letters
>   Personal invitations to visit for free consultations or information
>   Follow-up notes to thank prospects for their time

Assimilation
>   Customer welcome messages
>   Thank-you notes for purchases
>   Activation incentives for new customers
>   Incentives for future purchases

Cultivation
>   Special benefits and offers to high-value customers
>   Card and/or gifts for personal milestones or seasonal holidays
>   Referral requests and follow-up thank-you notes
>   Thank-you notes or e-mails following orders
>   Newsletters with value-added content
>   Offers to drive top-of-mind awareness during high activity time frames (back to school, holiday, spring/home improvement, etc.)
>   Usage incentives
>   Customer satisfaction surveys
>   Targeted cross-sell information

Reactivation
> Service recovery messages
> Intervention contacts with reasons to stay with the company
>> (based on attrition modeling)
> Acknowledgments that customers are valued and missed
> Activation incentives for inactive customers
> Notes letting customers know "the door is always open"

Sender/Recipient Relationship

As important as what a message says and when it's received is *who it's from*—especially when it's positioned as a personal message from a representative of an organization.

When a megacompany CEO sends a letter to a far-removed customer, the savvy recipient is undoubtedly clued in to the fact that the "personal" message is just one of thousands or millions created by automated printing—not personally written by the CEO. On the other hand, a well-timed thank-you note from a local salesperson to that same customer *is* meaningful.

That isn't to say an emotion-based message from the top is never appropriate. In Emotion Marketing there are three levels of sending: many-to-one, few-to-one, and one-to-one. The approach should be appropriate to the specific sending situation and the stage of the customer/company relationship.

For example, a beautifully designed and carefully chosen holiday card from the national office is a perfectly appropriate way for even the largest company to reinforce its brand identity and express appreciation for customers' loyalty. The card is a reminder that even at the highest level, the corporation is dedicated to meeting customers' needs.

An office, branch, store, or division might thank customers for their business or send information about specific new products or additional services that might be of interest. A note or call from an individual within the company is the right approach for service recovery efforts, follow-ups to meetings, and other highly personal touchpoints.

Choosing the appropriate level of sender makes the contact more meaningful; varying the sender by touchpoint encourages the recipient to form an emotional bond with the brand—not just an individual. That way, if that individual moves on, the customer still has a reason to remain loyal to the company.

One additional comment: Not all organizations are structured in a way that permits all three levels of sending. For example, long distance carriers or credit card issuers typically have centralized communication functions, not local offices or individual reps assigned to a given customer. So they're limited to many-to-one sending.

> *Choosing the appropriate level of sender makes the contact more meaningful.*

There are still techniques, however, to make these communications more personal and meaningful. *Storytelling within the communication tends to humanize the organization.* The use of a spokesperson or character also makes communications more personal. And something as simple as signing a card or letter from an individual rather than "Company XYZ" makes the contact more meaningful.

Frequency

The more frequent the communication, the more impact it can have on the relationship. When Hallmark tested frequency in the Gold Crown Card Program, it discovered that incremental communications to selected segments were both profitable and cost-effective; tests of fewer mailings resulted in decreases in store visits and buying behavior.

Of course, companies can go overboard. Constant e-mail updates, for example, become easier and easier to delete. Incessant reminders of a customer's importance may be taken for granted at best and at worst may seem insincere. And constant mailings on every product or service a company offers imply minimal respect for the recipients' Energy and failure to focus on their needs.

Additionally, the frequency of communication should vary by customer segment to maximize the return on the marketing investment. As a rule of thumb, a company's highest value customers should receive more frequent contact than less profitable customers. The Hallmark Gold Crown Card Program communicates with their best customers monthly; less frequent shoppers are contacted on average every other month. This ensures that the marketing resources are allocated toward high value customers and away from lower value customers. The net results are a bigger bang for the buck and higher ROI.

Perceived Value

Similar to the frequency of contact, the perceived value of each contact should be proportional to the value of the customer. Every contact, regardless of customer profitability, must have a baseline minimum value to the recipient: in other words, it must be relevant. Each contact must be perceived by customers as valuable and worth their time—not just intended to make a contact or plug a product. But beyond a baseline, the value of a contact can vary by customer value.

For example, during the holiday season, lower value Gold Crown Card customers might receive holiday postcards, while core customers might get greeting cards, which have higher perceived value. High value customers might be sent gifts—holiday music CDs or ornaments—along with their holiday cards.

Another common example occurs in the nonprofit sector; higher donation amounts typically qualify the donor for higher value gifts. All contacts have *some* level of perceived value and help build the donor relationship, but the perceived value increases as the value of the donor to the organization increases.

As mentioned, some contacts must be purely dedicated to relationship building, without a request for a response or transaction. These communications tend to have a very high perceived value because there's no quid pro quo, no hook, no strings attached. And the value customers perceive is *emotional* value: the sense that they are appreciated as an individual—not just as a customer.

A good rule of thumb is one relationship-building message for every two transactional touchpoints. The sequence of messages also is key: Customers are more likely to purchase—and do it more often—from companies with which they feel an emotional connection. So it's important to "sow before you reap" and build the relationship first.

ADDING EMOTION TO DIRECT MARKETING COMMUNICATIONS

The marketing strategy for a contact or series of touchpoints is just the beginning—solid creative strategy and execution make the difference between a piece that feels contrived or insincere and one that evokes an emotional response.

Hallmark Loyalty Marketing Group has developed a tool—the Relationship-Building Scorecard—with criteria for evaluating direct marketing for emotional value. The scorecard is used for every touchpoint the group creates and in analyzing existing elements of a clients' communication stream. These creative criteria are used in addition to assessing technical direct-marketing attributes, e.g., the list and segmentation, the offer, and the response mechanism.

The analysis begins with a basic question: What is the emotional intent of the piece? Once the goal of the contact is established, the following attributes are rated:

> *Relevance:* Is the piece something the recipient would expect to receive from the sender? Will it be welcome? Is it likely to enhance the relationship?

Clarity: Is the purpose of the contact obvious? If a response is desired, are the expectations clear?

Consistency: Does the piece reflect the sender's brand identity/image?

Mutual benefit: Does it offer value to the sender as well as the recipient?

Creative concept: Is it engaging and memorable? Is it unique and differentiated? Is the content compelling?

If a given contact gets a low score on some or all of these attributes, the opportunity to exchange emotional value may be wasted. And worse, the message may create distance instead of strengthening the connection.

SELECTING COMMUNICATION VEHICLES

Emotion Marketing calls for integrated marketing communications that meet the five guidelines listed above. Those communications can come in whatever form makes sense—postcards for sales promotions, e-mails for updates or helpful information, a phone call to check satisfaction with a recent purchase.

From the consumer perspective, direct mail is particularly effective in meeting the tactical requirements of an Emotion Marketing strategy. The Harte-Hanks' National Study of Customer Loyalty found that *customers prefer to hear about new products and services by direct mail—it's preferred by 87 percent over personal visits, phone calls, or e-mail communications.*

And even more specifically, personal letters, notes, and greetings are ideal vehicles for emotion-driven messages. The Customer Loyalty study revealed that:

- Fifty-two percent of respondents said a company that "notices loyalty and sends a thank-you letter and gift" would strongly encourage them to be more loyal.

J. C. Hall *on* Finding the Right Message

from *When You Care Enough,* published by Hallmark Cards, Inc., 1979

While we certainly give a lot of attention to the graphics and design of our cards, we are just as concerned about the message—or, as we say, the sentiment. A well-known axiom around Hallmark is that a card is picked up by a customer for what it looks like but is purchased for what it says—which determines whether it serves its purpose or not.

Writing sentiments is a highly specialized skill. The general opinion is that it's easy. Writers in other fields especially assume that greeting card sentiments can be dashed off in the shower. We receive as many as 2500 freelance submissions a month and publish less than one percent of them.

What a sentiment says is extremely important, but even more important is how it's said. With few exceptions, sentiments should not be long and should be understood immediately. People who have the ability to say what they feel simply and in a pleasing way are the best greeting card writers.

Often people say they don't want sentimental cards. But our experience is that they will choose the sentimental card when it's properly done. Greeting cards are sent to special people in their lives, for whom they have strong feelings—parents and relatives, sweethearts and friends. These intense relationships require sentimental language.

A good sentiment writer must be able to put himself in the position of both sender and recipient. In judging cards we often ask, "What is its sendability?" The best-written sentiment and the handsomest design are meaningless if they don't fit a sending situation. Since there are millions of senders and receivers, we have to determine the most effective combinations of sentiments and designs. All of our cards are compared on a sales basis in thousands of stores and run through our computers. One of our greatest assets is our file of tested and proven sentiments.

Over many years of experience, we have found that the vast majority of greeting card buyers prefer verse to prose.* One reason may be tradition. The first published sentiments were in verse, which became so well established that a greeting card did not seem to be a greeting unless it rhymed. Probably another reason is that verse is more difficult to write and adds value to the greeting. Also, verse is recognized as romantic language—and more appropriate to occasions for sending cards. People can express emotions in verse that might seem embarrassing in prose.

We publish prose, of course, in our humorous contemporary line, many sympathy cards, Christmas greetings and cards for men. We've also introduced more prose in cards directed to young adults, illustrated with soft-focus, romantic photography.

People ask me who writes our sentiments. In fact, over the years, I've often been asked if I was a writer or an artist. People assume I must be one or the other—but I am neither. I have never drawn much more than a straight line, and I've never even tried to write a sentiment. The overwhelming majority of our sentiments are written by members of our staff. They are a talented and prolific group. It is tough work, but it's very rewarding. Our writers see their work published on millions of greeting cards that reach many more millions of people, since each card is shared by at least two individuals—and usually more.

*In recent years, card buyers have come to prefer shorter, more conversational prose sentiments, according to Hallmark research.

- Sending a letter and gift after an inconvenience strongly encourages 46 percent of respondents to remain more loyal.
- A company that simply "notices loyalty and sends a thank-you letter" would strongly encourage 37 percent of respondents to be more loyal.

Within the direct mail arena, personal correspondence makes the most impact. Mail observation research conducted for Hallmark[36] found that personal greeting cards and letters are anticipated, opened first, and read thoroughly:

- Nine in ten participants looked forward to receiving personal letters and greeting cards—it made them feel that they're important to someone else.
- None of the personal greeting cards received were intended to be discarded without being opened—resulting in a *100 percent open rate.*
- A majority of participants agreed that a handwritten address is the primary indication that a mail piece is going to be personal and special.
- Advertisements and credit card solicitations are the most common type of mail participants discard without opening.

The amount of personal mail Americans get is on the decline. A U.S. Postal Service study showed that of 22 pieces of mail received each week, only 1.2 pieces are personal—down from 1.6 just 10 years ago.[37]

Customers are more inclined to be loyal when they know their business is appreciated—that someone cares. And personal mail is a *very* effective way a company can show it cares.

Cards and letters are as key to relationship-building in the business world as they are in people's personal lives. They work for small businesses as well as Fortune 500 companies, allowing "mass" emotional messages to

J. C. Hall *on* the Power of Greeting Cards

from *When You Care Enough,* published by Hallmark Cards, Inc., 1979

During World War II when there was a dire shortage of paper, the government dismissed the greeting card industry as nonessential in issuing priorities for paper. Edward L. Bernays, a legendary public relations executive, was engaged to develop a plan to inform the public and the government of the importance of greeting cards, especially during wartime. Before the study, Bernays himself regarded greeting cards as simply a novelty with no social significance. He learned some things we didn't know ourselves—or at least hadn't thought about.

He found that greeting cards were one of the most important means of personal communication. Over half of all personal correspondence was represented by greeting cards, and they had taken on even more meaning with so many people separated from their families. The survey showed that greeting cards were a much needed way of expressing deeply felt sentiments during trying times. It is not easy for most people to write sentimental or sympathetic letters even under normal circumstances. Greeting cards were the natural substitute. Bernays concluded that greeting cards were a major "factor in building the morale of the people. . . . I have no doubt about the useful purpose they serve in a society in which there are now millions less lonely because of them."

As a result, greeting cards were in much greater demand during the war than ever before. Women had always been natural users of cards—now men who had never sent them before turned to them in droves. The two great wars, which separated families around the globe, broadened the custom of sending greeting cards.

We realized many years ago that ours was a sensitive business. The shared sentiment a greeting card represents opens lines of com-

> munication that might otherwise be closed. A greeting card can cre-
> ate, enhance, and often rebuild friendships and associations.
> Samuel Johnson once wrote: "A man, Sir, should keep his friend-
> ships in constant repair." This has become increasingly difficult in
> our complex and mobile society.

be perceived as one-to-one communication. They communicate caring. They can be used for touchpoints across the entire Emotional EKG.

And they fit with the three Emotional Es:

Customers are more inclined to be loyal when they know their business is appreciated—that someone cares.

- Equity—for developing and reinforcing trust
- Experience—for enhancing exchanges and interactions
- Energy—for contacts convenient for the customer

REAL RESULTS

For service recovery issues, Hallmark's consumer affairs unit used to send an apology letter with a $25 gift certificate. A few years ago they switched to a beautiful, hand-signed "goodwill card" without a certificate. The impact was immediate—repeat purchase behavior was actually higher for customers receiving the card without a gift certificate. And Hallmark began receiving dozens of thank-you cards in response. By using more personal, emotion-driven communication, Hallmark reduced costs, increased sales, and built customer loyalty.

Across a variety of industries, Emotion Marketing pioneers are seeing overwhelming results—tripled response rates, doubled average dollar transactions, and in one case a 10,000 percent ROI. Following are a few Emotion Marketing success stories shared by Hallmark Loyalty Marketing Group clients; each incorporated emotion-based messages and offers into an existing, customer-focused program.

Major Insurance Company

This company knows from experience that its best new customers come through referrals from existing customers. But rather than a standard "Hey, thanks for your business—and by the way, would you send me a referral?" letter, Hallmark Loyalty Marketing Group and the company followed the Emotional EKG and created several touchpoints:

- Following a positive experience with a customer, the agent sent a thank-you card to the customer, expressing appreciation for his or her business. Tucked in was a business reply card requesting names of anyone who might be interested in assessing their insurance needs. Each card included a "handwritten," personal note, printed in a font that actually replicates the agent's own handwriting.
- After receiving a referral, the agent sent the customer another note—this time a simple thank-you for the referral.
- The agent then sent an introduction card—including a personalized résumé and "handwritten" note—to the prospect.
- After closing the sale, the agent would send a "welcome" contact to start building the customer relationship immediately, with the hope that one day this customer would be loyal enough to give a referral of his or her own.

The program was tested against a control group, which received a standard letter and reply post card. The segment that received an emotional greeting card returned *235 percent more* referrals.

The success of the program depended on the agents, who had concentrated on building emotional connections with their customers all along. Without the relationship, the cards would seem insincere and the program would net mediocre results at best.

Telecommunications Company

In business for fourteen years as a wireless provider, this company was accustomed to "churn," the telecommunications industry term for customer turnover. Their efforts were focused on acquiring scores of new customers, instead of keeping the existing ones. No emotional connection existed between customer and company—the only contacts in the communication stream were bills and sales materials.

About three years ago the organization made the switch to Emotion Marketing. Recognizing that customers typically left after 11 months, they developed an anniversary program; high-risk customers were targeted based on their time with the company and segmented based on their projected value. Along with an anniversary card, each top customer received a 60-minute calling card; the second tier got a 30-minute card; and a third tier received a 10-minute card. The lowest-value group received an anniversary card only.

The company's goal was a five percent drop in churn—*the overall result was a 13 percent reduction.* A subsequent two-tiered mailing resulted in 12 and 10.5 percent rates, respectively. The simple addition of emotion-driven communication generated increased loyalty—even in an industry known for fickle customers.

National Credit Card Issuer

The majority of credit card customers with past-due balances can, and even want to, make payments. But for a variety of reasons—guilt, avoidance, fear—they don't look forward to calls from customer service representatives. In an era of answering machines, voice mail, and Caller ID, avoiding contact is easy.

One major credit card issuer had statistics proving payment arrangements could be made with the majority of those customers if the reps could only get in touch. And since the company dedicates significant resources to credit counseling and providing assistance, it wanted to let people know the goal wasn't just collecting the money, but also winning trust and confidence—and keeping customers.

They targeted customers who had been unreachable and had accounts from 75 to 125 days delinquent. Hallmark custom-designed a card with a warm, sincere, supportive message encouraging the customer to call the company. It was mailed in a handwritten envelope with a first class stamp, and included a personalized, handwritten salutation, signature, and phone number.

The result? *An over 10,000 percent return on investment, and millions of dollars in collected revenue* that otherwise would have been written off as bad debt—not to mention freeing company resources from collections efforts. The card issuer said it was one of the most effective and profitable mail programs it had ever seen. A key to success was the treatment the customers, often tentative or emotionally overwhelmed, received when they finally called the company. The communication had to be consistent, and it was vital for the customer service reps to be as understanding and friendly as the message in the card.

National Retail Bank

The competition to become "card of choice" is fierce. Credit card issuers are constantly trying to acquire new cardholders, activate dormant accounts, or increase usage among lower activity cardholders. Debit card issuers want to capture an increased share of transactions, primarily as a replacement for cash or checks. In both cases, the goals of increasing activation and usage rates are significant challenges that, if met, pay off handsomely.

In two different programs—one for credit card and one for debit card customers—a national bank tied a premium offer to usage levels. The premium was presented with an emotionally engaging message, selected for high perceived value and uniqueness, positioned as a gift, and tied to usage requirements varying by segment.

Once again a careful Emotion Marketing strategy paid off with even higher-than-expected results: The credit card usage and activation program drew an *18.5 percent response rate.* The debit card usage program generated a *44 percent response.*

Both programs succeeded in part because of a compelling offer and strong creative message. Segmentation and targeting also were critical success factors.

National Department Store Chain

One retail chain's birthday program evoked emotional responses so strong that the marketing manager whose name appeared on the envelope received stacks of thank-you cards in response. Many were friendly and even chatty—clear indicators the nationally recognized brand made a personal connection with its customers.

The goal of the program was to generate incremental store traffic and transactions—and to reward high-value customers for their loyalty. The birthday card was accompanied by a coupon for 10 percent off any purchase during the birthday month; it drew a response rate lift of 25 percent, and average transactions were more than double those of the control.

The department store called the initiative its most successful direct marketing program ever. It provides more proof of the power of personalized contacts and the effectiveness of a carefully targeted communication program. And it goes to show that customers want to be loyal, but their loyalty must be earned.

TO SUM IT UP

- Communication is the highway used to exchange emotional value. Emotion Marketing is impossible without a robust, ongoing, two-way dialogue with customers.
- Effective Emotion Marketing communications are personal, relevant, relationship-focused, intended to create an emotional con-

nection, unique, and differentiated. The communication stream should include functional, rational, and emotional contacts.

- The five key elements of an Emotion Marketing communication piece are:
  1. Relevance
  2. Timing
  3. Sender/recipient relationship
  4. Frequency
  5. Perceived value
- The Relationship Building Scorecard rates direct marketing creative based on:
  1. Relevance
  2. Clarity
  3. Consistency
  4. Mutual benefit
  5. Creative concept
- Cards and personal letters are effective relationship-building tools because they allow "mass" emotional messages to be personalized and perceived as one-to-one communication, they communicate caring, and they can be used for touchpoints across the entire Emotional EKG.

CHAPTER NINE

Emotion Marketing on the Internet

"The Web is informational, it's not emotional—[and] has not yet taken its place among the major vehicles of persuasion."

Lester Wunderman
Founder, Wunderman, Cato, Johnson[38]

The Emotion Marketing chain of events has been established and defined: Profitability is driven by loyalty, and loyalty is achieved largely by building emotional relationships with best customers.

Once solidified, these relationships *comprise an enormous competitive asset*—one so pervasive and powerful it could literally dwarf other line items on a balance sheet. Because after a person has bonded with a company, it often requires too much time, energy, and risk to defect to a competitor. Just think of a pediatrician who has served a family's medical needs for years, and the lengths that family would go to in order to avoid switching doctors and starting a relationship from scratch.

A company beginning to build emotional relationships needs a couple of primary ingredients. One, obviously, is information. Who *are* a business's best customers in the first place? Where are they? What do they

Once solidified, customers' relationships comprise an enormous competitive asset—one so pervasive and powerful it could literally dwarf other line items on a balance sheet. Because after a person has bonded with a company, it often requires too much time, energy, and risk to defect to a competitor.

buy—what do they value? How do they shop? How are they motivated? And on and on. A second basic requirement is the means to reach these people—effective communications that deliver relevant messages in timely, meaningful ways.

A tool to accomplish both these needs is readily available to businesses and consumers alike: the Internet. Marketers, though, have yet to harness its true power.

To date, companies have used the Internet in a limited capacity, primarily as an online catalog and one-way communication tool. In restricting the medium to a transactional role, they have only taken advantage of a small slice of its range. Slowly, web sites are evolving into more than just places to put and retrieve information. They're becoming two-way and multiway communication vehicles. They're tools to both simplify and expand. They're places to learn, grow, and bond.

But they still have a long way to go.

WHY LOYALTY ON THE WEB IS IMPORTANT

Internet commerce is exploding—on the steep edge of a curve that's getting steeper. At the end of 2000, about 135 million Americans, over half the population, will be Internet users.[39] Online business-to-consumer retail sales will increase to $144 billion by 2003—a sevenfold increase in just four years.[40] E-tailing will certainly never replace traditional storefronts or catalog shopping. But as today's teenagers and preteens settle into their buying habits, they'll no doubt rely on the Internet more than older generations who had to overcome doubts and discomfort before hopping online.

The idea of loyalty may seem anachronistic in a high-tech environment, where people are valued for their "eyeballs" and attention spans are shrinking. But surprisingly, retaining customers by building emotional relationships is more important online than in traditional venues.

Recently, Frederick F. Reichheld and Phil Schefter examined the loyalty factor online, trying to corroborate results found in traditional retail outlets.[41] They asked: Are profits on the web as sensitive to customer retention as they are in other channels? Does the loyalty model (high investments to acquire and acclimate new customers, followed by high returns and rewards to serve stable customers) hold up in the electronic world?

> *Does the loyalty model hold up in the electronic world? The answer is an emphatic yes. The benefits of e-loyalty are, in fact, even more pronounced than in the physical world.*

The answer is an emphatic yes. The benefits of e-loyalty are, in fact, even more pronounced than in the physical world. Acquisition costs, Reichheld and Schefter concluded, "are considerably higher in e-commerce than in traditional channels. In apparel, new customers cost 20–40% more for pure-play Internet companies than for traditional retailers with both physical and online stores."[42]

But while acquisition costs are higher on the web, the *payback* to a business is also greater. "In future years," the authors continue, "profit growth accelerates at an even faster rate. In apparel e-tailing, repeat customers spend more than twice as much in months 24–30 of their relationship than they do in the first six months."[43]

Altogether, an enormous opportunity awaits Emotion Marketers who step up and capitalize on e-loyalty. Computer purchasers and online subscribers are creating huge potential for exponential growth, while most companies are, at most, just beginning to explore the Internet as more than merely a transactional, one-way communications tool.

These two factors have created an online environment charged with potential. The sites that are figuring out how to provide unique value, engage customers, and connect with them emotionally will differentiate themselves. Competitors may be just a couple clicks away, but customers will be protected from their offers by the personal investment an Emotion Marketer has made in them.

> *"Doing business online is about more than processing Web-based transactions. It is about using the Internet to develop, maintain, and manage positive relationships with customers, partners, and suppliers. The result is long-term relationships, repeat sales, business efficiency, and increased profitability."*
>
> Michael Dell
> Chairman and CEO, Dell Computer Corporation[44]

Industries accustomed to tracking which company is first-to-market with products or features will instead be watchful of something else: Which brands are first-to-market with the experiences that customers truly value? And which will be the first to *receive* loyalty because they've been eager to *give* it in the first place?

THE INTERNET TODAY

The Internet was first developed to link scientific and academic researchers, giving them the ability to relay messages, data, and programs. When commercial sites appeared, their intentions and strategies were markedly different. Yet instead of breaking out and creating unique properties all their own, web sites simply adhered to the Internet's existing transactional nature and lack of intimacy. Too many marketers took an offline paradigm and force-fit it onto the web without any truly special adaptations. As a result, e-commerce today has an abundance of *potential* energy. Like a coiled spring, it's waiting for a force such as emotion to impact it and set it in motion as a radically different, almost unrecognizable medium.

Take points-based rewards systems like MyPoints.com or ClickRewards.com. They do a good job of encouraging customers to visit partner sites, but are still learning how to leverage the unique capabilities of the Internet. And like points-based loyalty programs in the traditional world, they haven't followed through yet on nurturing emotional connections. The tools to do so are present, though—the technological ability to gather a world of demographic and behavioral information, then deliver customized, relevant messages.

Internet advertisers are having an equally difficult time bonding emotionally with consumers. Offline, marketers succeed regularly in creating trust and Equity using ads across a variety of media. But on the web, banner ads often trick or manipulate people into clicking on them. Net surfers, who at one time responded to the ads and saw them as a novelty, have disengaged and become bored. People now perceive them as an intrusion and virtually ignore them. Standard click-through rates on banner programs are down to just tenths of a percent, and marketers also find that few people pay attention to their e-mail ads.[45]

Meanwhile, most standard e-commerce sites have not yet evolved past being an online catalog. Companies have done a good job minimizing the number of clicks and making the checkout process secure, but few have broken free from the paradigm of merely presenting merchandise and offering a convenient way to purchase it. Marketers should be asking themselves what their sites can do to connect emotionally—to find out not only what products their visitors purchase, but what experiences, services, and information they truly value.

A few sites have been pushing beyond the online catalog mindset. Williams-Sonoma.com shares recipes with its regular visitors.

Amazon.com provides book and music reviews, and makes product suggestions based on customers' past purchase behavior. And pet product supplier Petopia.com offers a "bottomless bowl" option: Customers designate the kind of food their pets eat and how frequently they need a new bag, then Petopia makes automatic shipments so people don't have to worry about perpetually ordering.

Companies like this are adapting because they *have* to. The intense pressure of surviving online has led businesses to reexamine their strategies. They realize they can't always be in a mode to sell, sell, sell, which is a powerful temptation given that so much e-commerce is driven by price. Sites like the ones above have put a stake in the ground: They are using new techniques to nurture loyalty and create a sustainable, competitive advantage. Emotion Marketing principles will help bring their efforts to the next level.

BRINGING EMOTION TO E-COMMERCE

Online companies, like their offline counterparts, must manage the rational and emotional components of the Value Star^{SM} differently. To enter a marketplace, they need strong Product and Money platforms—that is the cost of entry. But a company can't rely on these rational components in the long run, for they can be duplicated or beat online even more easily than in the physical world. Quick, easy shopping comparisons force web sites to ensure their Product and Money is at least in the neutral zone and not a disadvantage. Equity, Experience, and Energy may seem old-fashioned, but in the end they will be the features that differentiate the winners. They'll be the reason web sites are bookmarked and moved to the top of favorite lists.

> *"The 'e' doesn't stand for electronic; it stands for emotion."*
>
> Kevin J. Roberts
> Chief Executive of Saatchi & Saatchi PLC[46]

There are no off-the-shelf solutions to add emotion to Internet experiences. Companies are still learning how to use the medium to create compelling value and build strong relationships with customers. Marketers *are* testing the waters, though, and are gradually discovering ways to shore up e-loyalty. Here are some ways companies can make it happen.

Know why a customer is visiting. First and foremost, companies must recognize what motivates people to go to a site, then develop the site with those drivers in mind. Businesses have an enormous opportunity to either simplify or expand what they offer on the Internet—they must make that call based squarely on what consumers demand.

For instance, if consumers simply want to know the address of a hotel they've booked or what to do if they've inadvertently misused an over-the-counter medicine, the web site should respect those needs. It should be easily navigable, getting people in, around, and out of the site as effortlessly as possible, leaving out banner ads, unnecessary links, and slow-to-download graphics. "Stickiness" is *not* the goal in cases like these, and any attempt to make visitors stay longer than they need will frustrate—even anger—them, leading to a loss of trust and Equity.

If, on the other end of the spectrum, a person turns to the web to explore a passion like golf or movies, then a business can load the site with facts, stories, entertainment, pictures, videos, sound, you name it. People in this mode may even *welcome* advertisements and links to other commercial sites.

Simplifying or expanding a site based on consumer intentions is an important first decision, because it impacts nearly every other step down the road: content, architecture, navigation, design, etc. This strategy decision is also critical because it shows visitors that the company understands them and cares about the Energy they spend. These messages begin to form an early foundation of the relationship.

When appropriate, add content. Content is key. It heightens the overall experience of browsing a site. In the new economy, where many outlets offer interchangeable products, services, and information, companies must rely on other content solutions to separate them from competitors.

The Internet is a two-way, interactive tool—marketers should take advantage of this capability to discover just what kinds of additional content consumers yearn for. One way is to simply ask visitors about their preferences. Another way is to put a variety of content out there and see what draws responses from people. Content possibilities include:

- customer testimonials and ratings
- access to a community or chat room
- product recommendations
- chances to "ask-an-expert"
- tips on how to use or enhance the product
- entertainment

Outdoor equipment supplier REI uses innovative content to appeal to their target customers' adventurous lifestyles. REI.com boasts 45,000 pages of data,[47] including clinics, checklists, glossaries, and unbiased product information covering a wide scope of outdoor activities. The company's commitment to providing information and feeding its customers' passions is a key differentiating factor, placing it on an altogether higher plane from its competitors.

Businesses will also benefit by continually refreshing the content their site offers. New information, product, and services perpetually revitalize a site, stirring customers and leading them to make repeat visits. This results in an enduring relationship and a deeper emotional connection.

Customize messages. Since the marginal cost of communicating via the Internet is essentially zero, businesses may be tempted to overdo it, blanketing their database with frequent messages, offers, and nuggets of information. While cost effective in the short run, this strategy is a poor Energy position to take. Customers' time is wasted, and their attention is distracted from the things they truly value. Overcommunicating is a signal to consumers that a company doesn't care about their time.

People are overwhelmed by what's offered on the web and are looking for companies to get to know them, understand what they value, edit the world for them, and present it in meaningful, exciting ways—*this* is what it means to customize messages. It's not just adding a person's first name to a variable text field—direct mail sweepstakes companies have been doing that for years. Customizing means collecting data regarding purchase behavior, shopping patterns, demographics, service inquiries, and the like, then putting all of it to use.

Marketers that deliver relevant, timely messages to consumers will accumulate a wealth of trust in their emotional bank accounts. As long as the companies offer a good rational value—solid merchandise and services at a reasonable price—consumers will return to them, because the brand name is winning on Energy.

To illustrate, imagine a woman who tries out an apparel site for the first time and orders a pair of cotton, khaki slacks. If the web site has chosen to compete on Product and Money, its main focus will be to sell her more stuff, regardless of whether she's interested. This customer can expect a flood of messages concerning unrelated products and untargeted offers. If, however, the company leads with Energy, it may send her a thank-you note, provide tips on how to dress the slacks up or down for different occasions, then let her know when the same product is on sale in a heavier fabric for fall. This respect for the customer's time demonstrates the company strives to know her on a personal level and is tailoring its communications to help make her life easier.

American Airlines' web site, AA.com, is on the leading edge of customizing messages to enhance relationships. It collects important information like travel frequency, home airport, and frequent destinations, plus it takes into account more unexpected data like the type of vacation customers enjoy and the hotel chains they prefer. This deep understanding of its customers lets AA.com send the right message to the right people at the right time. For instance, targeted customers in Plano, Texas, received special fare promotions to coincide with the local public schools' fall break.[48] Though the program is in its infancy, customers won't take long to learn that a communication from AA.com isn't just meaningless spam, but a relevant message containing a benefit that's sure to touch them directly.

Integrate the web site with other interactions and touchpoints.   A company may organize itself so its bricks-and-mortar stores, catalog, and web site all operate independently. But that structure is irrelevant and invisible to consumers. They expect a similar Experience across all interactions, regardless of the medium. And they want to feel confident that they're dealing with a single, seamless company, as opposed to being jerked back and forth among different channels. It's a tall order for businesses, but ultimately people will reward the successful ones with their loyalty, because an emotional connection has been established.

QVC's web site, iQVC, and LandsEnd.com both feature a remarkably convenient option where a customer service representative can be contacted online. A real-time conversation can take place—and a genuine relationship can be established—without forcing the customer to log off and make a phone call. Compare that to the e-commerce industry standard, where customers have to e-mail their service concerns to the company, then wait days for a response.

Eddie Bauer is another brand leading in Experience. As a well-integrated, clicks-and-mortar retailer, it lets customers make returns at any of its physical stores regardless of how they made their purchase. This saves people the hassle of repackaging merchandise sent from a catalog or online distribution center, hauling it to the post office, and paying for return shipping costs. And while at the retail store, the customers can also conveniently pick out the right size, color, or style to meet their needs.

Orchestrating interactions like this is a way to create a complete, satisfying Experience, one that shows respect for people's Energy and enhances their connection with a company. Satisfied customers, in turn, reward the brand with trust and Equity.

Create intrigue.   While the web certainly has limitations of its own, many of the physical and cost restrictions inherent in mass advertising or direct

Gold Crown Card Site Links Hallmark Retail Bricks with Hallmark.com Clicks

Hallmark.com and the Hallmark marketing group launched a new Hallmark Gold Crown Card section on the company web site in the spring of 2000, providing another avenue to serve the popular loyalty program's members. The alliance brings to life "bricks and clicks," a strategy linking in-store and online experiences.

Members of Hallmark's popular loyalty program receive personalized in-store offers, detailed account activity, previews of new products, program updates, reminders of important dates, and more. They can also earn bonus points by participating in online activities, such as providing their e-mail address or sharing things like ideas for creative kids' activities and favorite wedding memories.

Collected e-mail addresses and demographic data are used to create targeted communications (for customers who indicate their interest)—both in the mail stream and online—based on customers' product preferences and lifestyle/life stage. Members also receive personalized offers and incentives to visit Hallmark stores.

The goal of the "bricks-and-clicks" strategy is to use the online component to enhance consumer's experiences. The team works with other internal groups to ensure that marketing messages are consistent between retail stores and the Internet and continually looks for ways to add value through the Hallmark Gold Crown online experience.

mail are avoided by going online. Companies have the opportunity to be innovative, unique, even playful. They can excite people in all new ways and help impact how consumers perceive the brand name. Kevin Roberts, Chief Executive of Saatchi & Saatchi PLC, one of the biggest advertising agencies in the world, puts it this way: "You'll see a transition [on the Internet] from information to relationships. Great brands can't exist just by providing information. The great ones have mystery and sensuality."[49]

The cologne ckOne, a brand recognized for its edginess, uses e-mails to tell a fictional story, staging it as if it were real. The central character, a young woman named Anna, sends regular e-mails to ckOne's address list, writing about her boyfriends, family life, and adventures. Anna enhances intimacy by sharing secrets as if readers were her friends. The campaign is an intriguing, inexpensive way to build a brand image and could never have been delivered effectively via standard mail or traditional mass advertising.

Nike's recent television ad campaign is another great example of stretching the Internet. The athletic shoemaker broadcast action-filled commercials on TV, but stopped short of playing the conclusions, leaving viewers hanging as to how each ministry ended. Nike did make the final scenes available on its web site, though, where the company's net-savvy, early adapter target consumers could view them. While there, they could browse relevant products and services, including Nike iD, a build-your-own-shoe option.

Provide real value. The Internet's accessibility and technological muscle empowers marketers to really "wow" people and establish relationships like never before. In the early stages of the web, though, companies have mostly been using its unique properties to sell more goods. Strategies like this may or may not work. At best, they'll result in a quick, short-term revenue hit, but won't go very far in bonding with customers.

Consumers are searching online for much more than just product. They crave a brand to step out of the revenue-driving sales mindset, and instead get to know their needs and respond with genuine value and real benefits. People want a relationship and are delighted when a site offers things they can't find anywhere else and compelling reasons to return. In the end, people are delighted to give loyalty.

Take FranklinCovey.com. The company's main business is selling day planners and accessories, but its online Experience is far more enriching, appealing to people's emotional needs. They don't merely want to buy merchandise—they strive to take control of their lives, looking for ways to use their time more effectively and spend it on what matters most to them.

Franklin Covey understands this, and has responded with tools that satisfy people's basic human desires. The site offers an interactive program to help customers build personal mission statements. Visitors answer a few dozen questions, and within a minute or two they're presented with uniquely crafted principles and values to help guide their lives. Once the company has grabbed people with this emotionally driven advice, it can turn them into customers much more effectively—all the products to act on the emotional appeal are just a couple of clicks away.

Reflect.com is also a remarkably exciting and innovative site. Its emotional benefit is helping women feel more secure with their appearance and esteem. The brand's value proposition revolves around helping visitors understand their unique skin care, hair care, and makeup needs. When customers are ready to make purchases, Reflect.com doesn't display their products in a bland, uninspiring fashion. It romances the merchandise with striking graphics, provides personalized

> *In the early stages of the web, companies have mostly been using its unique properties to sell more goods. Strategies like this may or may not work. At best, they'll result in a quick, short-term revenue hit, but won't go very far in bonding with customers.*

advice on precisely what kinds of cosmetics would work best for customers, then directs them straight to those products. The company even offers buyers a choice of scents, colors, and packaging to fit their personality and integrate with their lifestyle.

> *Ultimately people are people, regardless of how they interact with a brand: face-to-face, over the phone, or in virtual space. As long as consumers are motivated most deeply by emotion, the Internet brands that touch and impact people will own the relationships.*

Clearly, FranklinCovey.com and Reflect.com are leaders in discovering and providing value. These companies earn trust and build Equity by putting consumer motivations first. "We understand you," they're telling customers, "and know your world is complicated. We want to help make it simpler by providing unique, relevant solutions that enhance your life." Instead of explicitly pushing product, they're solidifying one-to-one relationships. People will invest in FranklinCovey.com and Reflect.com because the companies have created a genuine bond with them. And they'll continue to invest because switching providers would require too much time and Energy.

THE WINNERS IN E-COMMERCE

Someday the turbulent phase of the Internet will subside. At that point some online brands will be leading the race and others will already be gone. It's of course too early to tell which companies will prosper, but the ones building genuine relationships with customers now will surely have a head start. These brands recognize that despite all the bargain hunters on the web today, Product and Money will only get them so far. Emotional content will be the fuel propelling the winners to the head of the pack.

Equity, Experience, and Energy will be the most important factors behind online success stories—much like in the traditional business world. Why the similarities? Because ultimately people are people, regardless of how they interact with a brand: face-to-face, over the phone, or in virtual space. And ultimately they're excited by benefits and value—things that can only be identified and offered through a genuine relationship.

As long as consumers are motivated most deeply by emotion, the Internet brands that touch and impact people will own the relationships. And these companies will have the loyalty—and the profits—to prove it.

TO SUM IT UP

- The benefits of loyalty on the web are even more pronounced than in traditional business. The costs to acquire a new customer are greater, but the payoffs from a mature customer are heightened as well.
- For the most part, though, marketers haven't yet leveraged emotion on the Internet. They've used it more as a transactional tool for one-way communications and uninspiring cataloglike product offerings.
- Online consumers yearn for a brand to speak to them as individuals. They want a company to take the world, edit it personally for them, and present it in a relevant way.
- Internet brands that win in the future will establish relationships with best customers. These companies will get to know their customers, and provide unique, compelling *value,* not just merchandise.
- Much like in traditional business, online companies need solid Product and Money platforms to enter a competitive marketplace, but they have to rely on the Emotional Es to win.

CHAPTER TEN

The Other E—Employees

They're the faces and voices behind every social exchange between a company and its customers. They're the people at the front lines of business relationships. They're the brand builders who hold the power to attract or alienate customers with every single encounter.

They're employees—the *other* Emotional E.

Gallup's Dr. Bill McEwen calls them the "fifth P" in the marketing mix—and says *a company's people "may well be the most powerful marketing resource available to build brand differentiation and enhance customer commitment."*

But he goes on to point out that people aren't as easy to control as the other Ps, "and that's critically important when setting out to assure a consistent customer experience."[50]

Brands exercise a great deal of control over every other aspect of the value proposition—whether its determined by the five points of the Value Star^{SM} or the traditional mix of Product, Price, Place, and Promotion. Products are designed, tested, and redesigned; pricing strategies are carefully calculated; merchandising, web sites, and other aspects of customer experience can be painstakingly plotted and managed; strategies and creative execution for advertising and other brand reinforcement are as much science as art.

But employees are people: independent, imperfect, uncontrollable, invaluable, *emotional* people.

> *Employee loyalty has never been more important to earn or been more difficult to come by. Many companies are recognizing the value of applying Emotion Marketing techniques to their internal customers—their employees.*

Fortunately, even though it's impossible to guarantee 100 percent perfection in interactions between employees and customers, companies can work the odds in their favor. *The Service Profit Chain* finds that in addition to the relationship between customer loyalty and profit, *the strongest connections are between employee satisfaction and customer satisfaction—and between employee loyalty and customer loyalty.*[51]

On the surface, strategies for building employee loyalty seem pretty similar to those for enhancing connections with customers; for example, the Value Star^SM model helps define meaningful offers (in this case, the total employment package), and the employee life cycle and Emotional EKG can predict commitment to a company. But there's one big, important difference: Customers spend a mere fraction of their time interacting with businesses. *Employees spend at least half of their waking hours at work.*

That means companies must provide value on more varied and deeper levels than they do for customers, and do so over a much longer period of time. Complicating matters further is the current corporate atmosphere—more than ever before, today's employees seem less likely and have fewer reasons to remain loyal.

The stakes have never been higher: Employee loyalty has never been more important to earn or been more difficult to come by. And there are many competing concerns for managers. But for the first time, many companies are recognizing the value of applying Emotion Marketing techniques to their internal customers—their employees.

THE BUSINESS CASE FOR EMPLOYEE LOYALTY

"It is impossible to maintain a loyal customer base without loyal employees."

Frederick Reichheld
The Loyalty Effect[52]

In the context of Emotion Marketing, the most obvious reason for a company to focus on internal relationship-building efforts is the connection between its customers and employees. The power of top-quality employees to differentiate a brand from the competition is easiest to see on the front lines: call center representatives, servers, flight attendants, retail salespeople, and others involved in daily customer encounters.

Lands' End has earned a reputation as one of the best direct merchants in the business based on the quality of its merchandise, its pricing, its guarantee, and its *people*.

"We believe that what is best for our customer is best for all of us," begins one of the Lands' End *Principles of Doing Business*. "Everyone here understands that concept. Our sales and service people are trained to know our products and to be friendly and helpful. They are urged to take all the time necessary to take care of you."[53]

It only takes a single experience with Lands' End to find out how completely and enthusiastically they execute those principles.

Southwest Airlines gets it, too. In an industry as likely to frustrate customers as any other, and in a company that openly touts its "no frills" approach, the employees are the stars. What other flight attendants' preflight spiels are forwarded in e-mails all over the Internet? ("In the event of a sudden loss of cabin pressure, oxygen masks will drop from the ceiling. Stop screaming, grab the mask, and pull it over your face. If you have a small child traveling with you, secure your mask before assisting with theirs. If you are traveling with two small children, decide now which one you love more.") And what other airline would encourage pilots to make jokes? ("We've reached our cruising altitude now, and I'm turning off the seat belt sign. I'm switching to autopilot, too, so I can come back there and visit with all of you for the rest of the flight.") Southwest's friendly approach gives passengers the feeling they're flying with old friends.

Front-line employees like these build customers' relationships with brands by using all three Emotional Es—they reinforce Equity, create Experiences, and maximize Energy. Workers benefit from these encounters, too; studies show the quality of customer interactions to be a significant driver of employee satisfaction and loyalty. A study by the authors of *The Service Profit Chain* found that in a banking organization "employees with highly satisfactory relationships with customers and attitudes toward their jobs had significantly lower levels of job turnover.

"This in turn resulted in employees developing: (1) a greater understanding of the requirements of their jobs (i.e., learning by doing), (2) enhanced teamwork and coordination within and among departments of the service organization, (3) enhanced knowledge of the needs of their customers, (4) a greater appreciation of the value of a highly satisfied customer, and (5) a better understanding of and commitment to key corporate goals and objectives such as that of improving customer satisfaction."

More pragmatically, the cost of high employee turnover is another incentive for businesses to make loyalty a priority. Remember that it's much cheaper to retain current customers than acquire new ones, and the same holds true for employees. Recruiting and training costs are just the beginning: *The Service Profit Chain* points out that loss of productivity and decreased customer satisfaction are even more significant expenses.

Losing certain employees can lead to customer defection. Insurance agents, sales people, attorneys, and other workers with long-term or highly involved customer relationships may forge such strong connections that these individuals become more important to customers than the brand, and clients will follow them whether they move to the competition or become the competition themselves, as free agents.

For employees who work "behind the scenes"—on production lines, in administrative positions, at headquarters—the connection between their satisfaction and that of the end users exists, but is more abstract. At Hallmark, for example, the marketing, creative, operations, and production teams must be as customer-focused, dedicated to adding value, and committed to "the Very Best" as any retail salesperson. The total value to the consumer comes from the combined value added by each employee. Where the link to customers is not clear to employees, however, the company bears the responsibility of creating a customer-centric culture. As Reichheld says, "The best employees prefer to work for companies that deliver superior value that, in turn, builds customer loyalty."

THE STATE OF EMPLOYEE LOYALTY

Corporate life would be simpler if commitment to customers was the only—or even most the significant—driver of employee loyalty. Unfortunately, today's working environment isn't as conducive to long-term employer-employee relationships as it once was.

Loyalty was dealt a major blow in the 1980s. Corporate mergers, downsizing, and layoffs made it clear that the implied employment contract, promising job security in exchange for life-long loyalty, no longer existed.

Once the shock wore off, workers responded by taking their careers into their own hands. *Fast Company* magazine calls one of the most visible elements of this new workforce the "Free Agent Nation." These consultants, freelancers, independent contractors, temps, and other transitory employees follow the lead of star athletes, selling their talent to the highest bidder.

This independent spirit infects full-timers as well. Whether they're disillusioned, restless, or unready to make a long-term commitment, some workers are simply interested in getting what they can out of an organization—knowledge, experience, training, résumé fodder—than in sticking around. For many, the new contract is a short-term commitment: a deal to exchange value and move on to the next opportunity.

People are able to job-hop now in part because the labor market is tighter than it's ever been. "Right now there are about a half-million people with high-tech skills in the marketplace and almost a million-and-a-half jobs to be filled," David Russo, executive vice president of human resources for BuildNet, told *Smart Business*.[54]

As the United States has moved from an agricultural to an industrial to an information society, workers have become less interchangeable. There's a premium on knowledge.

> *Companies must be more aware, more creative, more liberal, and more competitive than ever before to give those living assets a reason to return to the same job every morning.*

"A century ago the most valuable U.S. corporation was U.S. Steel, whose primary assets were smokestack factories," reads the introduction to the year 2000 list of *Fortune's 100 Best Companies to Work For*. "Today's most valuable corporation is Microsoft, whose most valuable assets go home every night. Companies that want those assets to return every morning must pay attention to the workplace."

No longer able to take loyalty for granted, companies must be more aware, more creative, more liberal, and more competitive than ever before to give those living assets a reason to return to the same job every morning. Just like customers, who benefit from unprecedented choice and information, today's workforce is in a position to demand more and more: high salaries and stock options, flexibility, perks, fulfilling work, and balance between personal and professional lives.

But employers who don't consider what they offer employees in the context of building long-term relationships will find themselves in the same awkward position as they might with customers. Workers drawn to jobs by bribes, from lucrative signing bonuses to BMWs, are the least likely to remain loyal. As Southwest's human resources VP, Libby Sartain, told *Smart Business,* "Buying the talent and paying whatever it takes never works. They never stay."[55]

Not to mention the fact that existing, experienced employees who watch new hires being offered better deals are now in perfect positions to offer their services to the competition. "The biggest challenge out there is not getting great employees—it's keeping them," according to an article entitled "The Hiring Crisis" in *Smart Business.* "The end of company loyalty also means the end of the stigma that used to be attached to changing jobs."

Hallmark's human resource department sums up the issues affecting loyalty with one word: diversity. Each employee has different priorities, and employers are challenged with accommodating an increasingly wide range of employee needs. But the deeper reason workers give their loyalty to employers is the same for everyone: The employer cares enough to provide something of value.

CREATING VALUE FOR A DIVERSE WORKFORCE

Hallmark Cards has a long-held reputation as a top employer. As early as 1927 workers received bonuses for each year they'd spent with the company. In the '30s, Hallmark instituted benefits unheard of in any industry, including retirement pensions, medical aid, life insurance, and vacation pay. By the mid-'50s, *Fortune* magazine called the company's benefits package "the country's most liberal employee-benefit and profit-sharing plan." Hallmark has appeared in *The 100 Best Companies to Work for in America* and a variety of other lists. Hallmark's 25-Year Club, which includes both current and retired employees, boasts 4500 members.

But as times change, other companies have begun to offer competitive benefits packages. A "one-size-fits-all" approach to policies and benefits that seemed appropriate in Hallmark's traditional operating environment may need to be reconsidered to meet the demands of 20,000 employees in a wide variety of disciplines and life stages. A culture that carefully guarded financial information and business decisions from the majority of employees is already changing, with the introduction of "learning maps" to educate all employees about the industry and the company's finances. In the '80s and into the mid-'90s, Hallmark employees were well taken care of, but inwardly focused and isolated from the consumer. The challenge for Hallmark as the company focuses outwardly on the consumer is to find ways to continue to make employees feel cared about.

At Hallmark—as with many companies—the drive to remain one of the best places to work and stay customer-focused are inseparable. No company is perfect, and there are many competing demands on the company, but providing a desirable workplace and being an employer of choice remain high priorities.

Emotional E: Equity Begins with Corporate Ideology

The first step in attracting and keeping the right employees is clearly defining what a company believes in, stands for, and works toward.

Much has been written recently about the need for employers to market to prospects and employees; the brand a company creates in the marketplace is an important reason why employees sign on and stick around. And just as brand Equity helps establish a connection between a company and its consumers, it serves as the foundation for its relationships with employees.

One of the ways to communicate a brand's promise to employees is in the clear statement of a company's values and purpose. "A clear and well-articulated ideology attracts to the company people whose personal values are compatible with the company's core values," James C. Collins and Jerry I. Porras write in "Building Your Company's Vision." "Conversely, it repels those whose personal values are incompatible."[56]

More and more, employees seek congruency in their business and

People Beliefs at Hallmark

Hallmarkers are committed to:	**Hallmarkers can expect:**	**Hallmarkers are expected to:**
Individual Dignity	A workplace in which everyone is treated with honesty, respect and sensitivity; and in which each person's full participation is sought and encouraged.	Work productively with each other; and to treat each other with honesty, respect and sensitivity for individual differences.
Performance	To work in a company where excellence is the standard; where meaning-ful work and clearly stated objectives support satisfac-tion of customer needs; where rewards reflect individual and business success; and where job opportunities are based upon consistently high performance and the willingness to adjust to changing needs.	To work collaboratively with fellow Hallmarkers to meet or exceed company standards; to participate in establishing aggressive objectives necessary to support ongoing success; and to contribute ideas for business improvement.
Communication	Direct, constructive and timely feedback on individual and business performance; consistent access to the information needed to do our jobs well; and the opportunity to be heard and responded to.	Accept and act on the feedback we receive; to engage in honest, constructive two-way dialogue with others; and to protect the confidentiality of employee, company and customer information.

Development	To receive information on the knowledge, skills and abilities the business needs to achieve its objectives; the opportunity to develop our fullest potential and an environment that promotes learning.	Take ownership of our own careers; engage in continuous learning to improve our personal productivity; and demonstrate consistently the skills needed to achieve Hallmark's business goals.
Fairness	The consistent application of our policies and practices with consideration of individual needs and circumstances.	Understand and apply the policies and practices of our company; and to work with appropriate Hallmarkers to make changes to those policies as business needs evolve.

personal lives. *Fast Company* reports, "People used to put on their 'game face' when they went to work. They became their real selves only when they returned home. These days, who you are—your experience, your attitude—overrides where you work as an index of your value."[57] Just as in personal relationships, employees are seeking employers whose values and cultures mirror their own.

Some core ideological points transcend industries. "The Hewlett-Packard Way" lists "trust and respect for individuals" and "uncompromising integrity" among its organizational values.[58] The owners of The Container Store, which ranked first on *Fortune's 100 Best Companies to Work For* list for the year 2000, say the company "has always seen its employees as its single most important element."[59] Merck values include "corporate social responsibility" and "honesty and integrity."[60]

Other value statements even more clearly define a company's character. Walt Disney's include:

- No cynicism
- Nurturing and promulgation of "wholesome American values"

> ## This Is Hallmark
>
> We believe:
>
> That our products and services must enrich people's lives
> and enhance their relationships.
> That creativity and quality—in our concepts, products
> and services—are essential to our success.
> That the people of Hallmark are our company's
> most valuable resource.
> That distinguished financial performance is a must,
> not as an end in itself, but as a means to
> accomplish our broader mission.
> That our private ownership must be preserved.
>
> The values that guide us are:
>
> Excellence in all we do.
> Ethical and moral conduct at all times
> and in all our relationships.
> Innovation in all areas of our business as a means
> of attaining and sustaining leadership.
> Corporate social responsibility to Kansas City
> and to each community in which we operate.

- Creativity, dreams, and imagination
- Fanatical attention to consistency and detail
- Preservation and control of the Disney magic

Sony has valued "elevation of the Japanese culture and national status" and "being a pioneer—not following others; doing the impossible."[61]

It's unlikely an employee worth recruiting will be turned off by ideals like trust, teamwork, respect, or integrity. But Disney-specific values will attract idealists and dreamers and repel skeptics. Sony will draw innovators, and drive away hardcore patriots of any country but Japan.

Along with its values, a corporation's purpose can help draw in and inspire the right kind of employees for that business. Instigating social change, innovating, providing opportunity, improving the quality of life, and building relationships provide compelling, higher-level reasons to give loyalty to a company.

"Excellence happens only when people have a deeply felt sense of purpose in their lives," according to Gallup's *Workplace Column*. "Human beings want to belong to something that has significance and meaning. They want to know they are making a difference, and are contributing to an important endeavor."[62]

Emotional E: Experience Starts with People

One of the most common reasons an employee leaves a company is having a poor relationship with a manager. Although the company's ideology and vision are great tools for getting employees engaged, managers are the front-liners charged with building relationships with these vital internal customers. And just as employees bring companies to life for consumers, managers represent the strongest connection between an individual and an employer.

An employee may join Disney or G.E. or Time Warner because she is lured by their generous benefits package and their reputation for valuing employees. According to Gallup, great benefits and a reputation for treating people well might lure an employee to a company—but it's the relationship with his or her manager that will determine how long an employee stays and how productive he or she is.[63]

Gallup also found evidence of the importance of caring: In a list of 12 qualities that describe great workgroups, item five is: "My supervisor, or someone at work, seems to care about me as a person." And, just as it is in Emotion Marketing to customers, one of the best ways to show caring and improve Experience is to treat employees as individuals, seeking out and finding ways to meet their specific needs.[64]

Managers who inspire loyalty must be truly interested in helping people develop, and have the interpersonal skills to facilitate that process. Managers are no longer merely responsible for delegating tasks; they must mentor, inspire, and motivate employees to do what they do best. In short, all managers—from team leaders to CEOs—must lead.

AT&T CEO Michael Armstrong is lauded as "a real leader if there ever was one," in "Don't Hire the Wrong CEO," an article in the *Harvard Business Review*. Armstrong demonstrates extraordinary drive and technical know-how—but also something far beyond that.

"He demonstrates passion—love for his work and his people. His direct reports will tell you of Armstrong's warmth, empathy, and inclusiveness. They will tell you he cares. They will also tell you how natural it is to follow him."

Ironically, studies show motivating employees is simpler—and less costly—than some managers think. In one survey asking what workers wanted from their jobs, managers guessed their employees would rank good wages first, job security second, and promotion/growth opportunities third. The employees' preferences?

- Full appreciation for work done
- Feeling "in" on things
- Sympathetic help on personal problems

Job security and good wages ranked fourth and fifth with workers after these intangible, deeper needs.[65] Each of these employee motivators depends almost entirely on the managers' willingness to show caring—either by expressing appreciation, including workers in decisions and information, or showing concern for their personal lives.

Another survey reported the top motivating techniques as cited by employees, listed here opposite the percentage of time the techniques were actually used:

Personal thanks: 42 percent

Written thanks: 24 percent

Promotion for performance: 22 percent

Public praise: 19 percent

Morale building meetings: 8 percent

> *The relationship between a manager and a direct report provides daily opportunities for emotional connections, like giving feedback, recognizing good work, rewarding achievements— even simply spending a few minutes listening.*

The study concludes that four out of five of "the techniques that have the greatest motivational impact are practiced the least even though they are easier and less expensive to use."[66]

Opportunities to create value-added interactions with *customers* involve careful strategy; a single touchpoint may require a marketing, creative, and production team and weeks or months of planning. The relationship between a manager and a direct report, on the other hand, provides daily opportunities for emotional connections, like giving feedback, recognizing good work, rewarding achievements— even simply spending a few minutes listening. Even high-level executives—*especially* high-level executives—must habitually initiate meaningful encounters with their employees.

Emotion-based communication doesn't always have to work from the top down. When Hallmark studied the effects of one-to-one emotion-based communication in a business greeting card inundation study, participants discovered that some of the messages with the most impact were those they sent to peers or their own managers. Simple notes of appreciation, support, or caring provided two-way motivational Experiences; recipients felt valued, and senders felt good about making the effort.

Emotional E: Experience Through Flexibility

Today's workforce is mostly made up of Baby Boomers and Gen Xers. Sometimes regarded as opposing forces—stereotyped as the overachievers vs. the slackers—they share at least one common desire: flexibility.

Flexibility might mean shifting an eight-hour workday from nine-to-five to noon-to-eight. Or compressing a workweek to get Fridays off. Or job sharing. Or telecommuting. Or taking a leave of absence to travel to Europe.

Flexibility could mean allowing employees to move to different jobs, go on rotations, and experiment with new work styles, methods, or processes.

And flexibility might mean being empowered to make any decisions necessary to make a customer happy. Or the expressed trust and implied permission to change a workflow, go offline, create a new system, or do whatever it takes to get the job done.

Most of all, flexibility means the employer is willing to work with the employee to make the day-to-day Experience of the job a better fit *for the individual.*

One huge factor in the desire for flexibility is the need for work-life balance for every employee. In the past, those most concerned with balance were working moms; now it's equally sought by single and married people, straight and gay couples, traditional and blended families. Child care is still important; now, elder care is becoming more of an issue. And employees without dependents have work-life needs, too.

Achieving work-life balance used to mean compartmentalization—keeping eight hours a day strictly business and the rest purely personal. Now, more workers strive for harmony, expecting permission to deal with real-life issues at work and willing to check e-mail and voice-mail evenings and weekends.

"I used to think that what I needed to do was balance my life, keep my personal and professional lives separate," Susan Burish, a free agent who's spent much of her career in the corporate world, told *Fast Company.*

"But I discovered that the real secret is integration. I integrate my work into my life. I don't see my work as separate from my identity."[67]

Because of the variety and changing nature of employee needs, the challenge to companies is twofold. First, they must determine how much flexibility their businesses can tolerate and still meet external customer needs: Workers on a production line or customer service reps, for example, may have less leeway in setting their own hours than computer programmers or copywriters. Businesses must also decide how to meet the needs of a diverse workforce: Should they target a variety of segments with specific benefits and programs, or take on issues that cut across all segments?

It's a standard marketing quandary: Go after the niches or the common denominators? Emotion Marketing practices suggest creating Experiences as unique to employees' individual needs as possible within the larger context of the business.

Emotional E: Energy Means Workplace Perks

It wasn't always the employer's job to make its workers' lives easier. But across industries, winning the war for talent sometimes means going all out: Some employers have recently started offering concierge services to take care of errands, on-site child care, well-equipped employee gyms, dry cleaning, catered lunches, and other perks unimaginable just a few years ago.

A study by Watson Wyatt on attracting, keeping, and motivating employees confirmed that these "nonmonetary rewards *add convenience to employees' daily lives and engender higher loyalty.*"[68]

Offering value based on Energy can be as complex as setting up a computer, fax machine, and other home-office equipment—and providing training—to an employee who chooses to telecommute. Or as simple as offering a cell phone, pager, or laptop for personal as well as business use.

Some perks pay dividends beyond increased satisfaction and loyalty. Employers who provide fitness centers and wellness programs see long-term savings in health insurance and reduced sick days. Catered lunches and employee cafeterias keep employees on-site, increasing the time they spend working. And employees who aren't worried about children at day care or the lists of errands in their planners are more able to focus on their work.

The Rational Side of the Star: The Pay and the Job

Just as a quality Product and competitive Price/Money are the costs of entry to today's marketplace, a satisfying job and competitive compensation are minimum criticals for employee loyalty.

The Gallup *Workplace Column* list of the "12 dimensions that consistently describe great workgroups" includes such rational drivers as clear expectations, appropriate materials and equipment, and commitment to quality. But mixed in with the rational reasons are the emotional ones: the opportunity to do what an employee is best at, the sense that opinions expressed are valued, a best friend at work, and opportunities to learn and grow.[69]

Obviously, it's almost impossible to separate the rational from the emotional requirements when it comes to providing value through the Product; to most people, a job means more than just the series of tasks they perform or the place they show up to earn money.

The Money part, however, is a bit more quantifiable. These days, pay is more than simple wages—it may include bonuses, stock options, profit sharing, benefits, and other incentives proven to attract employees and help win loyalty.

"Since they've gone to the trouble of selecting only top performers, high-performance organizations don't 'nickel and dime' their workers," according to Watson Wyatt's findings. Sixty-five percent of organizations report above-the-market pay for critical skill employees, and 45 percent pay above-market for non-critical-skill employees.[70]

But—perhaps no longer surprisingly—Watson Wyatt and scores of other researchers have discovered pay isn't the most important element of employer-employee relationships: In one instance a vice president asked

Watson Wyatt to "fix his pay problem," only to find that though pay needed to be adjusted to be more competitive, the bigger issues affecting turnover and effectiveness were "leadership development, better training opportunities, and performance management."[71]

A Gallup report found that job stress and recognition share the spotlight with salary as the three most important drivers of employee satisfaction.[72]

Just as Product and Money are easy for competitors to duplicate in the marketplace, jobs and wages alone won't differentiate a company in the eyes of recruits and employees. The intangibles—Emotional Es like the culture, relationships with managers and coworkers, and demonstrations of corporate caring—are the factors that distinguish a good company from a great one and move employees beyond mere satisfaction to loyalty.

USING THE VALUE STAR^{SM} AND EMOTIONAL EKG TO BUILD RELATIONSHIPS

Just as Emotion Marketing allows businesses to build relationships with specific consumer segments, as well as with individual customers, applying its principles within the workplace can help strengthen relationships with employees on a variety of levels.

At the macro level, especially in larger corporations, it will be necessary to research employee opinions and desires. Hallmark frequently surveys its employees to understand their opinions. A current survey seeks to find the relative importance to Hallmarkers of factors like compensation, leadership, accountability, variety, and, of course, flexibility.

Companies can also make some generalizations based on specific workgroups—creative employees, engineers, working mothers, and computer programmers, for example, may require more flexibility in scheduling and work styles than operations or finance. And traditional, more reliable methods of compensation may prove more relevant to older workers than Internet-economy-focused new hires.

This high-level approach to using the Value Star^{SM} to add value for

Nurturing Creativity

It's easy to see why enhancing the *customer's* Experience is important. But what about *employees?* They're the ones who manage consumer interactions, create the products, and facilitate the services—so providing an enriching, engaging, invigorating work environment just makes sense.

Hallmark's 700-member creative staff is accountable for generating more than 30,000 greeting cards and other products each year. From the beginning, founder J. C. Hall understood the value of nurturing this invaluable human resource; years ago he sent his son Donald to look for ideas at newspapers, ad agencies, and at the company belonging to his father's friend, Walt Disney.

Don Hall Sr. discovered there was no set method or list of rules. "But the common thread was that you cannot leave an artist alone for too long. They need a good deal of attention and nurturing and renewal."

Hallmark's illustrators, artists, designers, writers, editors, and photographers face the everyday challenge of applying strategy to paintings and poetry, and channeling passion into products that meet customer objectives. To spark their creativity and encourage innovation, Hallmark provides access to a wide variety of resources, which include—but are by no means limited to:

- Kearney Farm. Formerly a working farm, this 300-plus acre spread now serves as a working retreat for Hallmark's creative and business communities. It includes a spacious, refurbished farmhouse that supports brainstorming sessions, business meetings, and creative exploration. A lake, nature trails, and wildlife add to the ambience.
- Creative Workshop Rotations. Small teams spend up to six

months focusing on a particular trend, printing process, or new technology; they might study laser technology, spirituality, storytelling, or specific consumer groups. The sessions are comprehensive and intensive; teams share their results by creating videos, presentations, and product prototypes.

- The Barbara Marshall Award. The award grants creative employees salaried and fully funded sabbaticals to explore or further develop areas of interest or expertise, followed by a show of their work. One artist explored the creation and costuming of porcelain dolls, right down to dyeing all of her own fabric and hand-painting the dolls' faces. Another traveled across the country in pursuit of technique, color, and knowledge of light; working on his own time schedule (sometimes around-the-clock) and from his front porch, he produced 20 exquisite six-by-nine-foot paintings.

- Creative U. Part of Hallmark's Creative Resource Development Group, Creative U sponsors learning and development programs that align with corporate strategies—product leadership, for example—and support creative job-related competencies—from technological proficiency to emotional articulation. Classes, presentations, forums, and tours include everything from "Painting Techniques: Floral" to "Elements of Voice" to "Beyond Conflict to Collaboration."

employees can be compared to consumer database segmentation. In the future, parts of the employment package, like benefits, programs, and policies, may be based on demographic, lifestyle, and attitudinal characteristics—along with specific job requirements and duties. The intent is to build an enduring relationship between the employee and the company as an entity—not just to the profession, a department, or a manager.

As complex and extensive as they may be, individual employees' priorities are at least far easier to ferret out than customers' needs. Contact

J. C. Hall on Hiring the Right People

from *When You Care Enough,* published by Hallmark Cards, Inc., 1979

One of the most frequent mistakes made in hiring people is to confuse ability and affability. Now affability is a wonderful trait, but if it's not accompanied by ability, it doesn't amount to much. Of course, it is extremely important to sell yourself. People have to believe in you and get along with you. But if your opinions are contrary to theirs, you've got to have the courage to say so whether it's popular or not.

I also think an excellent employee will work harder for rewards other than money. He'll put a sense of accomplishment first—and the money will take care of itself. If you show a well-intentioned individual just what to do and set a good example yourself, he'll get along just fine. A more difficult lesson, and one that took a little longer for me to learn, is: The sooner we get rid of someone who makes no effort to do a good job, the better. However, I always found that talking about this idea was much easier than executing it.

As a boy I had read an article about R. H. Macy's program of hiring and training people, and I continued to read about Macy's employment practices. They inspired me as our business grew. Macy's was one of the leaders in developing policies—such as training programs—that led to successful personnel operations.

Time and again I was told that large industries hired people for as little money as possible and worked them as hard as they could. Little consideration was given when people were ill. The belief was prevalent that treating people too well spoiled them.

In this regard I often found myself in disagreement with our supervisors. One night I had two extra tickets to the theater. I suggested to the office manager that we give them to someone who had been doing a particularly good job. He felt it would only spoil the person who received them and suggested I give them to a relative or friend, which I did reluctantly. I was irked with myself for this decision.

Shortly after that, I had a long visit with my next-door neighbor, Joe Dawson, who taught me an important lesson in handling people. Joe had retired after many years of supervising people at the Wells Fargo Express Company. He found that established practices of constantly watching over people and reprimanding them for the slightest infraction were not productive. The best results were obtained by simply treating people decently and expecting the same in return.

can be almost constant, opportunities for learning take place hourly, and emotional connections can occur on a variety of levels: department to employee, workgroup to employee, manager to employee.

Most business groups have built-in opportunities to measure priorities—performance reviews, 360° surveys, and regular staff meetings, to name a few. But some of the most critical information is obtained through one-on-one interaction: daily discussions between coworkers, diligent listening by managers and mentors, and straightforward discussions about wants and needs. All of these things are much more likely to occur, incidentally, in a culture that supports listening and rewards managers who invest in employee development.

As it does in the consumer world, the Emotional EKG can add depth to management's understanding of its relationship with employees across their life cycles. Employees have different relationship needs—and varying levels of emotional commitment—as they move from recruitment and hiring (acquisition) to training and their first experiences as employees (assimilation), through their careers (cultivation), and through rough spots or resignations (reactivation). Some points to consider at different phases:

- *Acquisition—recruiting and hiring*

    Remembering that a compelling job and competitive pay are minimum criticals for recruiting, keep in mind that the Emotional Es allow a company to differentiate its identity and its offer from the competition and attract the kinds of employees more likely to remain loyal.

Successful companies look for the intangible value in their prospects, as well: In *The Service Profit Chain,* Rosenbluth International CEO Hal Rosenbluth says, "It's not technical skills we're looking for, it's nice people. We can train people to do anything technical, but we can't make them nice."

Southwest Airlines' CEO Herb Kelleher echoes the sentiment: "Hiring starts off looking for people with good attitude—that's what we're looking for—people who enjoy serving other people."

- *Assimilation—training and early experiences*

Just like customers, new hires find themselves at the fork in the relationship road: Companies can spark loyalty or inspire apathy. Hallmark's training programs and orientations, both company-wide and in different divisions, focus on more than just information about job skills and protocol—they get leaders involved in communicating the company's vision, engaging employees in the mission, and drawing them into the corporate culture.

- *Cultivation—the career phase*

In this phase, experienced, committed, empowered employees are most valuable to a company and its customers. They're potential evangelists, capable of spreading the corporate gospel to

> *As complex and extensive as they may be, individual employees' priorities are at least far easier to ferret out than customers' needs. Contact can be almost constant, opportunities for learning take place hourly, and emotional connections can occur on a variety of levels.*

both customers and potential employees. In fact, some companies find that employee referral programs are their best sources
for finding new recruits.

This is also the phase for Peppers and Rogers' Learning
Relationship; a company can increase its understanding of the
employee's needs and make adjustments to better meet them.

Employers must be careful not to take dedicated employees
for granted, or lose sight of their contributions and potential as
business needs change. Because the current corporate climate
doesn't always foster long-term commitments, quality employees willing to give their loyalty should be treated like the invaluable resources they are.

- *Reactivation—from rough spots to resignation*

Employer-employee relationships aren't always smooth
ones—burnout, dysfunctional teams, conflicts, stressful projects, and other issues crop up even in top companies. But quick
and caring resolutions to problems can cement a valuable
employee's loyalty to managers and the company as a whole.

Sometimes, employees need more support than even the
best of managers can provide, and an employee assistance program staffed with professionals can help with reengagement.
Hallmark has also developed a program called "Compassion-
ate Connections," where employees who have gone through a
personally difficult time, like battling cancer or losing a child,
can help other employees experiencing similar difficulties.

In today's transitory work environment, losing some of the
best workers is inevitable. If a former employee is beginning
life as a free agent or freelancer, there's opportunity for a continued relationship.

And it's not a bad idea to keep the door open, allowing
workers to return when appropriate: Companies can save
training costs and gain employees less likely to stray again. Not
surprisingly, most come back for emotional, deeper-level rea-

sons: flexibility, security, people, or commitment to a company's purpose.

COMMUNICATING WITH EMPLOYEES

Using the Value Star^{SM} to understand priorities can guide a company in creating or enhancing its value proposition to employees. And using the Emotional EKG can help gauge workers' emotional commitment at various stages of the employee life cycle.

Strong employer-employee relationships require the same elements as those with customers—only in larger doses. Mutual benefit, commitment, authenticity, and communication are vital components. And once again communication, on a variety of levels, is an essential means of imparting the other components.

As in the consumer arena, a company sends employees both informational messages—memos, forms, e-mails, voice-mails—and emotional ones. For the emotion-based touchpoints, all the same elements are important: relevance, timing, sender/recipient relationship, frequency, and perceived value.

Of course, employees receive far more information communications than a customer. So carefully delivered emotional contacts are guaranteed to be particularly effective and appreciated. Again, the Emotional EKG is an excellent starting point for creating a communication plan.

Acquisition
> Introductory letters
> Personal invitations to visit the office or corporate campus
> Follow-up notes to thank potential employees for their time

Assimilation
> Welcome messages
> Support and encouragement through training and "new kid"
> > phase

Congratulations on completion of training or learning new skills

Cultivation

Recognition of career and personal milestones

Card and/or gifts for birthdays or seasonal holidays

Congratulations on achievements

Notes to say hard work was noticed

Reminders that the company is lucky to have such a loyal employee

Appreciation notes

Newsletters and updates

Rewards for achievement and extra effort

Sympathy and "Thinking of You" messages during personal hardships

Reactivation

Apologies for conflicts, problems, or mix-ups

Reminders that managers are available to listen and help

Encouragement or support through difficult times

Congratulations on moving on

You'll be missed

"Thinking of You" messages

The added benefit of emotional communications with employees is the opportunity for spontaneity. Hallmark research shows that some of the most appreciated messages are the unexpected ones: the "Way to Go!" card in a mailbox or the gift certificate for the extra hours an employee thought went unnoticed.

Of course, the one-to-many, CEO-signed holiday letter is a welcome gesture, too. And the surprise department trip to a baseball game is just as appreciated as the meticulously planned anniversary celebration. The important thing is the effort—and the sincerity behind it.

"A lot of this is golden-rule kind of stuff," Marc Drizin, a vice president at Walker Information, told the *Wall Street Journal*. "Do people ask

Communication in a Caring Culture

As in any large corporation, Hallmark relies on extensive internal communication to inform, inspire, engage, and motivate its 20,000 employees. But perhaps more than in most companies, emotion-based communication plays just as important a role as purely informational messages.

- *Noon News* is a daily publication distributed throughout Hallmark's headquarters and plants. It features articles on company objectives, new products, stories about our subsidiaries, and consumer information, as well as weekly want-ads, and announcements of anniversaries, retirements, promotions, weddings, and births. Because of Hallmark's foundation in publishing, *Noon News* is—and probably always will be—ink on paper, but now is also available on the company's intranet site.

- *Hallmark Intranet* is an ever-expanding internal resource. Employees can access basic information, like a company directory, their pay stubs, and the "Crown Room" cafeteria menu. In addition, various divisions support their own sites, such as research's often-updated "Voice of the Marketplace" and an events and entertainment calendar sponsored by the creative community.

- *CEO Forums* allow small groups of employees, typically fewer than 50, to meet with CEO Irv Hockaday and raise business questions and concerns. Quarterly *Town Hall* meetings allow Hallmark leadership teams to present high-level information to all employees, and promote enthusiasm about and understanding of business fundamentals.

- *The Hallmark Monitor* broadcasts information, including retail performance updates and news items, during regular work hours. Each plant location can feature local news and pick up feeds from headquarters.
- *The Hallmark Retailer*, a monthly publication, and the "Hallmark Gold Crown News," a bi-monthly video, provide forward-looking sales and product information, business strategies, tips on productivity, and other relevant information to retailers.
- *Greeting cards* are, not surprisingly, a ubiquitous means of celebrating special events, cheering on coworkers, expressing support, and recognizing effort. Employees receive a 50 percent discount on all greetings in on-site card shops—free business-related cards are also provided to encourage peer-to-peer recognition. Employees receive cards for birthdays and anniversaries from management teams; Don Hall sends an annual Thanksgiving letter, and his family sends a customized holiday greeting (see pages 193 and 194).

me how I'm doing? Would the company help if I had a personal emergency? Does it provide family-friendly benefits? Do people pay attention to how I feel at work? And are they developing me for the long-term, not just for the current job?"[73]

By following Emotion Marketing principles, employers can make sure the answer to each of those questions is an unqualified yes.

Hallmark Cards

DONALD J. HALL
CHAIRMAN OF THE BOARD

November 15, 1995

Dear Hallmarker:

As we stop to think about 1995, it will undoubtedly be remembered as a year of enormous challenge and change. But it has also been a year of much progress.

Although there is much more to be done, we have taken the all-important step of reaffirming our commitment to product leadership. That is, and has always been, the key to our company's success.

Today, with the right people in the right places, I believe we are moving forward with a renewed sense of excitement and purpose. We are in position to make our company much stronger for the future.

In the midst of all of this activity and change, we don't want to lose sight of the things that are so important in our lives -- our families and friends, the freedoms and opportunities we enjoy, the satisfaction of jobs well done.

During the next few days, as you celebrate with friends and family, set aside the day-to-day bustle of business and be mindful of the joy that your blessings bring.

I offer a special prayer of thanks for you and for the many ways you are working with other Hallmarkers to embrace change while remaining committed to the fundamental principles that guide our business.

My family and I thank you for your talent and enthusiasm, and we wish you a happy and restful Thanksgiving.

Sincerely,

Don

HALLMARK CARDS INCORPORATED · KANSAS CITY, MISSOURI 64141 · (816) 274-5111

Figure 14

Hallmark Cards

DONALD J. HALL
CHAIRMAN OF THE BOARD

November 17, 1993

Dear Hallmarker:

Thanksgiving is a time for reflection. And undoubtedly, one of our most vivid memories of 1993 will be the Midwest floods. But Thanksgiving is also a time for renewal. And although the floods brought obvious devastation, they also brought an opportunity for rebirth.

The flooding definitely reminded us of the power of nature and the vulnerability of human communities. Although they tested our stamina, the floods highlighted our ability to care for one another, and they gave the rest of the country a glimpse of the Midwestern values upon which our company was founded. Resilience, neighborly spirit and enduring good humor in the midst of disaster sustained many families, including Hallmarkers.

For many of us, the 1993 floods brought forth memories of similar flooding more than 40 years ago. It was July 13, 1951, when the Missouri River overflowed into Kansas City's industrial district, engulfing three major Hallmark warehouses with six to eight feet of water. Trees, trucks, and parts of buildings were flowing through the streets. The power of the flood was such that a railroad car weighing 23,000 pounds with a 50,000-pound load was washed away.

The resilience of those affected by the flood was incredible back then, too, and my father asked his friend Norman Rockwell to create a painting showing the strength and caring spirit of Kansas City people. The resulting painting "The Kansas City Spirit" came to symbolize the courage of men and women who put service above self.

Challenge, it seems, often brings the best in us forward. I am proud of the many ways Hallmarkers accept challenges to help one another, strengthen our business and pursue individual goals. I am thankful for this company, what we represent in our communities and the thousands of Hallmarkers who believe in our company's special mission.

During the next few days, take time to cherish your loved ones and be thankful for one another. My family and I wish you a wonderful Thanksgiving.

Sincerely,

Don

HALLMARK CARDS, INCORPORATED · KANSAS CITY, MISSOURI 64141 · (816) 274-5111

Figure 15

TO SUM IT UP

- Customer loyalty is strongly linked to employee loyalty; employees play a critical role in building relationships between customers and companies.
- Whether they're on the front lines or working at headquarters, employees benefit from a customer-centric culture.
- Corporate downsizing and layoffs, the growing number of "free agents," and a tight labor market are a few factors that make earning employee loyalty more difficult than ever before. Employers are challenged with accommodating an increasingly wide range of employee needs.
- Establishing clear corporate ideology plays an important part in building a company's Equity and in attracting and keeping the right employees.
- Managers represent the strongest connection between an individual and an employer; strong leadership adds value to an employee's Experience with an organization.
- The need for flexibility, due in large part to workers' desire for work-life balance, is one of the biggest challenges facing employers today.
- Energy-based perks that make workers' lives easier are effective in attracting employees and inspiring loyalty.
- A satisfying job (Product) and competitive compensation (Money) are minimum criticals for employee loyalty.
- Using the Value Star^{SM} to understand priorities can guide a company in creating or enhancing its value proposition to employees. And using the Emotional EKG can help gauge workers' emotional commitment at various stages of the employee life cycle—from recruitment and hiring (acquisition), to training and their first experiences as employees (assimilation), through their careers (cultivation), and through rough spots or resignations (reactivation).

- Emotion-based touchpoints—planned and spontaneous—are especially effective in building relationships with employees because of the high number of informational communications they receive daily.

CHAPTER ELEVEN

Emotion Marketing—
An Action Plan

S ome companies are fortunate.

From the beginning they've built caring into their cultures. Whether they put a name on it or not, emotion is an integral part of doing business. And strong relationships with customers *and* employees increase and enhance their successes.

Many profitable businesses benefit from their use of emotion-based value drivers, but in most cases fail to optimize the potential of the Emotional Es. Emotion Marketing clarifies the basic principles behind creating lasting, caring relationships with customers. The Value Star^{SM}, the Emotional EKG, and the Relationship Building Scorecard prove effective tools for creating and evaluating loyalty programs.

Before diving into an Emotion Marketing initiative, it is important to be reminded of a few points. Emotion Marketing:

- is not a stand-alone strategy
- won't mask unhealthy relationship practices
- calls for a long-term commitment to customer relationships
- needs top-down support and a caring corporate culture
- requires continuous effort at all levels of the company

Standards of Excellence

In 1985, Hallmark adopted this formal creed:

Excellence
For us excellence is an aspiration
an attitude,
a pursuit,
a way of life.

Excellence is all of us
working together, aspiring to
the fullness of our potential
always in pursuit of higher
standards—determined to do
everything we do somehow better
than it ever has been done before.

Excellence is found
in the caring,
in the trying,
in the doing.

It is our objective. We seek it
with dedication. It is the hallmark
of this corporation.

Chapters 1 through 10 built the case for Emotion Marketing with theories, principles, and examples. This chapter offers recommendations for making Emotion Marketing a reality in any company; it's followed by a series of client-tested assessment tools for evaluating every factor in the value equation.

The Hallmark Loyalty Marketing Group follows a four-stage action plan—a continual process with a feedback loop to the beginning after each full cycle. Its stages are:

- Assessment
- Strategy
- Implementation
- Evaluation

Before launching a campaign, it's critical to determine how an Emotion Marketing program will align with the company's mission, high-level strategic initiatives, and financial objectives. Senior management buy-in is essential to success; winning approval is easier when proponents can clearly articulate the ways Emotion Marketing not only supports but strengthens core corporate strategy.

> *Before launching a campaign, it's critical to determine how an Emotion Marketing program will align with the company's mission, high-level strategic initiatives, and financial objectives.*

STAGE ONE: ASSESSMENT

The process begins with an assessment of the current state of a company's relationships with its customers. After pulling together existing customer research and other information from relevant databases (e.g., customer database, call center reports, and web site activity reports), marketing strategists can determine what additional customer insights might be needed and conduct research to determine:

J. C. Hall on Selling Ideas

from *When You Care Enough*, published by Hallmark Cards, Inc., 1979

Several years ago Richard Deems, chairman of Hearst's Magazines Division, was visiting us. We were discussing a meeting I'd had that day, and I expressed concern that our people weren't sure our objectives were attainable. I felt that if they just believed they could be accomplished—they would be. But for some reason people resist new ideas.

Dick said this was a common experience in publishing as well. He had a drawing in his office of the Wright Brothers' plane, *Kitty Hawk*. It showed the figure of a man talking to Orville Wright—with the caption: "It won't fly, Orville."

That seemed to sum up the whole problem to me. With Dick's permission I had some tent cards printed with this message. I kept one on my desk for many years. When anyone told me something couldn't be done, I pointed to the card. I had been trying to say the same thing in many more words all my life.

It reminded me of a statement by General David Sarnoff, the dynamic founder of RCA who was a wizard in electronics. At the dedication of a new science building at Princeton University, he said: "Any intelligent man who has watched color television and has seen a jet plane take off would have to believe that anything the mind of man can conceive can be accomplished."

On another occasion, talking with Dr. Norman Vincent Peale, he turned to me and asked, "What is the biggest problem you have in your organization?" I said, "Selling ideas." Now, Dr. Peale is one of our most successful ministers and writers, and he replied wearily, "My job is selling, too, and I just have to keep working at it all the time."

> And I recall President Eisenhower saying that his greatest problem was selling ideas—to his staff, to his cabinet, to Congress, and, ultimately, to the American people. Winston Churchill was one of the greatest salesmen who ever lived. He sold the Free World on arming itself, probably the most important selling job ever accomplished.
>
> Selling ideas is the most crucial of all jobs. Essentially it is getting people to think your way. In that sense, I've been selling all my life.

- What customers want and value from the organization
- How customers currently perceive the organization

Customer satisfaction is the most commonly used relationship measure. But a more comprehensive tool is something Hallmark calls the *Caring Index:* a tracking mechanism that measures the degree of emotional attachment at a deeper, more meaningful level than mere satisfaction. As research by Hallmark and others has shown, *when customers feel a company genuinely cares about them, they're exponentially more likely to give their loyalty.*

As its name implies, this index gauges how cared-for customers feel at various stages in the relationship. With the Value Star^{SM} as a guide, it's possible to focus questions on different points. For example:

Equity: Does the company have your best interests at heart? Does the company share your values? Would you feel comfortable recommending the company to friends? What is your level of trust?

Experience: Is the shopping environment engaging? Are the customer service reps attentive and helpful? Is it pleasant to interact with the company, regardless of the distribution channel?

Energy: Is the order process easy? Are the locations convenient? Does the company respect and value your time?

When conducting this kind of research, it's also important to keep in mind the subconscious nature of motives, and probe for unarticulated

J. C. Hall on Meeting Customers' Needs

from *When You Care Enough,* published by Hallmark Cards, Inc., 1979

It troubles me that there's a great compromise with quality in America today. This has affected us adversely in all walks of life—in the education of our children, the conduct of our government, the manufacture of our automobiles, the design of our houses and commercial buildings—and even in the movies we see and the television we watch. There has been an increase in shoddy craftsmanship in America and less pride among the repair trades. Public services have declined. Deliveries arrive late or damaged—and often the wrong item is sent. Is it any wonder that the consumerism movement has become a great force in this country? It may be too critical at times, but more often it's right. Its success has clearly demonstrated a need. And manufacturers and retailers should take it seriously and apply it constructively. When the consumer speaks, we'd better listen.

In part, our rapidly changing times have brought about this compromise with quality. Things have moved too fast for people to change them. No wonder young people are baffled and looking for different answers—and hopefully better ones. But, too often, they find worse ones.

Another factor that has encouraged the compromise with quality is the increase in mergers and conglomerates. There haven't been too many organizations combining forces to improve quality. Some of them do, but the ones I hear about are those that only want power and profit.

There is not only more need, but more opportunity today for better draftsmen, legislators, educators, television, and products and services of all kinds. We have the new technology to build on. It shouldn't make us lazier or less inventive. It should be a boon to creativity. And up to the point we are willing to pursue it, it can release us for more time to improve the quality of our endeavors and our lives. It will take great courage and enthusiasm. America can furnish all of this and more. We will, if we care enough.

needs to discover opportunities for meeting those needs in new or unexpected ways.

Once the Caring Index is established, companies are able to measure changes in feelings of emotional attachment over time, and use their findings to predict future purchase behavior.

Another standard element of preliminary research is an inquiry into brand image and customer perception of the company's intended brand identity. In establishing early benchmarks, the most comprehensive approach is to use the Value Star℠ on each of its three levels.

The first level *compares the company to the competition* on each of the five value drivers, plotting each organization's strengths in the areas of Product, Money, Equity, Experience, and Energy. Next, from the perspective of the *customer,* the company is rated against competitors on each point—will customers perceive a clear competitive advantage, a disadvantage, or parity?

At the next level, research helps predict each of consumer segment's priorities. After combining perception analysis with psychographic variables and life-stage information, it should be possible to determine the relative importance of each value driver. For exam-

> *Once the Caring Index is established, companies are able to measure changes in feelings of emotional attachment over time, and use their findings to predict future purchase behavior.*

ple, time (*Energy*) may be the primary value driver for a working mom. But a retired couple may be less concerned about time and more driven by trust (*Equity*) or price (*Money*) for a particular product category.

Once priorities for different groups are understood, the segments can be mapped on the Value Star^{SM}. This exercise indicates how well an organization's competitive strengths and weaknesses align with the needs of their target segments.

Finally, technology has allowed even the biggest companies to understand customers' needs on an individual level. Every company probably has focus group research indicating what hundreds or thousands of customers think in aggregate. But what does each one of them want? By beginning to track and learn individual motives, a company can find out how well it's meeting each of those needs over time.

If there's no existing means of discovering individual needs on the points of Value Star^{SM}, there's clearly an opportunity to dig deeper and find out more.

To Recap

1. Assemble existing customer research and other data.
2. Conduct additional research as needed.
3. Assess strengths and weaknesses relative to competitors on each of the five points of the Value Star^{SM}.
4. Assess relative importance of each value driver to each consumer segment (and ideally to each individual customer).
5. Identify gaps where customer needs are not currently being fully met.

STAGE TWO: STRATEGY

Following an assessment of the overall value proposition against the competition and customer perception, the next stage requires developing strategies to bolster perceived value by capitalizing on strengths and overcoming weaknesses and value gaps.

The most effective strategies start from a position of power, leveraging strengths to take advantage of key opportunities rather than trying to overcome weaknesses to avoid competitive threats.

Obviously, addressing both strengths and weaknesses is necessary for value optimization. *But the best way to springboard into Emotion Marketing is with a value driver that customers perceive not only as their most important need, but also as one of the company's greatest strengths.*

As an example, a hotel whose customers give it high marks on *Experience* but low ones on *Energy* might begin by targeting guests who are willing to go out of their way for the ideal environment, rather than going after a new audience by changing its format to be more convenient.

Based on the competitive assessment and customer research and segmentation, a company can determine value gaps and decide which ones to bridge and which to ignore. This is the time for marketers to evaluate the relative attractiveness of each segment and select target groups.

If a segment is desirable, then the company must be able to win on the drivers those customers value the most. The relative size and profitability of each segment helps establish the appropriate level of resource investment. If a company wants to attract working moms, it must win on *Energy*. For example, if wealthy empty-nesters are the target, and research shows trust and a set of shared values are the primary value drivers, a company must build its *Equity*.

Segment attractiveness hinges on the amount of money customers are spending with a company and in the total category—in other words, the company's share of wallet. The conceptual model shown on page 206 illustrates a basic resource investment approach.

Strategies, with accompanying objectives and metrics, based on each segment's value and potential value to the company, should be created with an eye toward allocating resources to meeting the customers' higher level needs.

Limited Potential Customer *Strategy: Maintain* Continue limited investment to sustain share	**High Value Customer** *Strategy: Honor* Invest for recognition and retention
Low Value Customer *Strategy: Ignore* No investment; divest if unprofitable	**High Potential Customer** *Strategy: Pursue* Add value to increase share

Current Value to Company →

Category Spending →

> *The key in Emotion Marketing is to communicate a willingness to serve the customers on their own terms.*

High Potential—Pursue

These consumers may be spending heavily in the category—but not on that company's brand. That means there's room for growth. By finding out what purchasers want and improving its value proposition to meet those needs, a company differentiates itself from others and can capture an increased share of this group's purchases. The key in Emotion Marketing is to communicate a willingness to serve the customers on their own terms.

High Value—Honor

This segment should feel the biggest impact from an Emotion Marketing campaign. They're the most likely candidates for what Peppers and Rogers call the Learning Relationship—a company can learn to meet their needs more easily and effectively with each transaction. They're the best source of profit for a company, a gold mine for referrals, and the most open to cross-sells. They should be thanked, rewarded, and treated like the valuable contributors to a company's success they are.

Limited Potential—Maintain

These customers may be spending their whole share of wallet with a company already. They're a steady source of revenue—but the level of business they'll do with the company has peaked. It's important to maintain this customer base—to meet their needs and communicate that they're valued—but to avoid overinvesting. By minimizing expenditures on this segment, more resources are freed up for the High Potential and High Value segments, leading to a higher return on investment.

Low Potential—Ignore

That may sound a little harsh. But this segment is unattractive due to low (or negative) profitability and little growth potential. Minimal resources should be spent against this group, because the return on investment will be low. Resources currently dedicated to marketing to and servicing the Low Potential segment can be reallocated to more attractive segments.

Planning the communication stream is the next step. As detailed in Chapter 8, communications should be targeted by segment, based on the earlier customer assessment of value.

Touchpoints for each customer during each stage of the Emotional EKG are more than just a way of conveying product information and promotions emotion-driven contacts make it clear that the company has created value for the customer *because it cares*.

Emotion Marketing messages say, "We listened. We took action. And now we're communicating with you about something we know is relevant, because you told us it is." For example, the primary message to a segment that values an engaging shopping experience should tout the excitement of the store atmosphere. Emotion can be leveraged through the communication plan regardless of whether the strategies being employed address rational or emotional value drivers.

No matter how perfectly integrated and flawlessly executed a communication stream might be, the message can get lost if the delivery is ineffective. A well-thought-out creative strategy can make the difference between a campaign that conveys the warmth and sincerity behind a company's relationship-building efforts and one that leaves the recipient cold.

Lastly, objectives and measurement methods must be determined to gauge the success of any initiative. Specific metrics, with corresponding time frames, should be created for each segment. In addition to providing an overall measurement of success, the metrics allow a company to evaluate success within segments and refine strategies as needed. The final section, *Evaluation,* discusses in detail the different measures of success for Emotion Marketing programs.

To Recap

1. Identify relative attractiveness of each segment.
2. Determine which segments to target and create strategies to leverage strengths and close value gaps identified in the *Assessment* stage.
3. Determine specific tactics to implement for each strategy.
4. Develop a communication plan.
5. Devise metrics and measurement methodology.

STAGE THREE: IMPLEMENTATION

Once the strategies are final and a communication plan is in place, the Emotion Marketing initiative moves into the *Implementation* stage, where tactics are executed and the touchpoint strategy is brought to life. While "executing tactics" sounds relatively straightforward, this is a significant effort and can make or break the strategy. This section won't attempt to reinvent the basic principles of effective implementation; however, it will highlight the factors most important to carrying out an Emotion Marketing plan.

In addition to implementing the specific tactics developed in the *Strategy* stage, internal organizational issues may need to be addressed.

One of the major reasons an Emotion Marketing initiative isn't easy to enact is the level of support required from every employee in the company, beginning at the top. In "Don't Hire the Wrong CEO" in the *Harvard Business Review,* authors Warren Bennis and James O'Toole point out:

> *Real leaders are great because they demonstrate integrity, provide meaning, generate trust, and communicate values. Real leaders, in a phrase, move the human heart. And there's the problem. The ability to move the human heart is difficult for most people to talk about—it's nebulous and squishy.*

The leaders who champion successful Emotion Marketing initiatives aren't afraid of talking about the squishy stuff. In 1944, Hallmark executives adopted the slogan, "When you care enough to send the very best." That boldly emotional statement reflected and helped solidify a corporate culture based on concern and respect for both the customers and the employees who produced the product.

For Emotion Marketing to work, human resources policies must be aligned with a focus on loyalty. Companies should:

- Write relationship-building principles into corporate beliefs and values—make them a dynamic part of the culture.
- Create a customer-centric organization structure.
- Make customer-focused behaviors a criteria for hiring.
- Continuously train and retrain employees to better anticipate and meet customers' needs.
- Set performance objectives and incentives around loyalty measures.
- Empower front-line employees to deliver superior customer service.

As mentioned in Chapter 4 (Experience), recognizing that employees are on the front lines of the relationship-building efforts may call for a significant reevaluation of a company's *employee* loyalty initiatives. Internal quality is measured by the feelings employees have toward their jobs, colleagues, and companies. Once again, *caring* is the bridge between satisfaction and loyalty. *There's a noticeable difference between satisfied employees at companies where they're just doing their job and employees who know their company cares about them.*

The headline of a recent *Wall Street Journal* preaches: "To Win the Loyalty of Your Employees, Try a Softer Touch." Findings of various employee-commitment studies name "such touchy-feely attributes as care and concern, trust, respect or fairness, as essential to building loyalty." In one recent study, "care and concern for employees, fairness and trust, are cited as the areas needing most attention: 56% of employees surveyed said their employers fail to show concern for them, 45% said their companies failed to treat them fairly, and 41% said their employers failed to trust them. Partly as a result, only 24% of employees are 'truly loyal' to their employers and plan to stay for at least two years."[74]

The fastest way to undermine a company's ability to win customer loyalty is to fall short in establishing an emotional connection with its employees.

For Emotion Marketing to work, all the elements have to come together seamlessly—connectivity, in the short term and over time, and through a whole series of transactions and communications, is a key to success.

To Recap

1. Execute tactics and communication plans developed in the *Strategy* stage.
2. Adjust internal organizational issues as needed (structure, performance management, staffing, and training).

3. Ensure appropriate I.T. infrastructure is in place to assist in adding customer value and measuring the effectiveness of the initiative.

STAGE FOUR: EVALUATION

Building loyalty is a long-term process and requires long-term measurements. Still, most companies demand proof of short-term success. In light of this paradox, comprehensive evaluation of an Emotion Marketing program should include three elements:

Short-term quantitative measures enable quick wins by tracking more immediate outcomes such as initial response, increased activation and usage, higher average transactions, successful cross-selling, etc.

Qualitative measures (like the Caring Index) tend to be attitudinal in nature and do not have a financial component. But they're leading indicators to measures that *are* financial in nature; customer satisfaction and loyalty measures are correlated to customer behavior and financial performance. Creating an emotional attachment today leads to the financial benefits of loyal behavior tomorrow and beyond.

Long-term quantitative measures ideally involve calculating customer lifetime value (LTV) and demonstrating the change to LTV based on implementing a loyalty initiative. Other long-term measures include retention, share of wallet (or share of customer), and ROI.

Customer attitudes and behaviors should be measured for each target segment, with attention paid to emerging trends. Measurement data can be used to draw conclusions about why program tactics succeed or don't, and this information can be used to refine strategies and tactics, creating a feedback loop within the process. Successful relationship-building campaigns require continual evaluation and refinement—the feedback loop allows companies to make each iteration more effective.

Building strong relationships is a long-term proposition. True loyalty isn't earned in a month or a quarter—but evidence proves the benefits are well-worth the investment.

> *Building strong relationships is a long-term proposition. True loyalty isn't earned in a month or a quarter—but evidence proves the benefits are well-worth the investment.*

CHALLENGES

Of course, any new initiative will encounter obstacles.

The most common challenge to proposing an Emotion Marketing initiative is the desire for a short-term gain. Companies zip out a thank-you message and immediately assess whether the program is successful or not. Or they change call-center scripting to be more emotional and look for an instant bump in sales. In many instances even the quick-and-dirty approach will net results—but for loyalty to stick, the effort must be ongoing. Trust isn't given on the spot; it's unrealistic to expect customers to go out of their way to be loyal after a single application of emotion.

Cost is another common issue. Some managers just can't understand making an investment in what they see as simply a "warm fuzzy." Fearful of throwing away part of the marketing budget, they might push to include traditional promotions, incentives, or offers. They want results. And the results are there, but complicated by the lack of a clear way to measure them. The connection between the Caring Index and financial performance is a relatively new concept.

Another challenge is the sheer scope of an Emotion Marketing initiative. So in the beginning it may make sense to kick off a comprehensive program by focusing only on the high-value customer segment. The program will be much more manageable, and wins with this group make it easier to sell an Emotion Marketing strategy that includes other segments.

More questions: How can a large organization translate Emotion Marketing to the individual level? When a database has five million names in it, what makes it personal and emotional? The answers aren't simple ones—they lie in carefully thinking through every element of the communication: the value proposition, its relevance, the creative execution. It takes practice to perfect. Part of the secret is in giving the brand a genuine personality—a distinctive voice, a recognizable look, and a real person customers can reach at the other end.

In any large organization it's a challenge to make Emotion Marketing work 100 percent of the time right off the bat. But communicating the philosophy over and over and over again, showing a high-level commitment to long-term efforts, and eventually receiving breakthrough results will make it an accepted part of the culture.

THE OTHER CASE FOR EMOTION MARKETING

A few years ago Hallmark studied Emotion Marketing on the one-to-one level with a business greeting card inundation study. Participants were asked to send five personal messages a week to clients, coworkers, and vendors.

Before the study, many of them expressed concerns that going so far outside the realm of standard business communications might be perceived as inappropriate, insincere, or even unprofessional.

But six weeks of sending individual, emotion-based cards proved their fears to be completely unfounded. Not only was such personal communication in the corporate environment appropriate, it was *appreciated*. It "jump-started" relationships in every stage of the customer life cycle.

And the positive impact wasn't limited to the recipients: The senders felt they were more attentive to their business relationships and that they were doing their jobs better. Because they needed relevant material for their personal notes, they paid more attention to people. They listened more carefully. They were better able to create friendships. They enjoyed their work more.

The service profit chain-driven, proven, *rational* business case for Emotion Marketing is clear. But the deeper reason for Emotion Marketing is—*emotional.* It's so simple, so basic, that it almost feels ridiculous to write it down: Doing business this way is the *right thing to do.*

Serving others satisfies our high-level spiritual and personal motivations. People typically meet those needs on their own time—through volunteering, church involvement, taking care of their families and friends. Emotion Marketing allows us to meet those needs in the last place we might expect to: at work.

In writing this book we struggled with the idea of how to "add emotion" to business theories and marketing principles. What would differentiate it from dozens of other books on loyalty and customer relationships? How would we talk to executives, but make it clear that it was coming from Hallmark?

Again the answer is simple: It's the right message, at the right time, to the right people.

"We wildly underestimate the power of the tiniest personal touch."

Tom Peters
Author and Management Consultant

That power can bring businesses closer to the customers they serve. It can make customers feel understood, valued, and taken care of. That *power* can transform mere work into something important and meaningful.

It's time to harness that power—the power of emotion.

TO SUM IT UP

- To help win approval from senior management for an Emotion Marketing initiative, determine how it aligns with the company's mission, high-level strategic initiatives, and financial objectives.
- Successful Emotion Marketing programs require a four-stage action plan. Its stages are Assessment, Strategy, Implementation, and Evaluation with a continual feedback loop back to the beginning.
- *Assessment* involves:

  Assembling existing customer research and other data.

  Conducting additional research as needed.

  Assessing strengths and weaknesses relative to competitors on each of the five points of the Value Star^{SM}.

  Assessing relative importance of each value driver to each consumer segment (and ideally to each individual customer).

  Identifying gaps where customer needs are not currently being fully met.

- *Strategy* involves:

  Identifying relative attractiveness of each segment.

  Determining which segments to target and creating strategies to leverage strengths and close value gaps identified in the Assessment stage.

  Determining specific tactics to implement for each strategy.

  Developing a communication plan.

  Devising metrics and measurement methodology.

- *Implementation* involves:

  Executing tactics and communication plans developed in the Strategy stage.

  Adjusting internal organizational issues as needed (structure, performance management, staffing, and training).

Ensuring appropriate I.T. infrastructure is in place to assist in adding customer value and measuring the effectiveness of the initiative.

- *Evaluation* includes:
  Short-term quantitative measures
  Qualitative measures
  Long-term quantitative measures
- Challenges to Emotion Marketers may include desire for short-term gain, cost, dealing with the scope of a relationship-building program, and difficulty translating mass communication to individual messages.

Assessment Tools

STEP 1: ASSESSING CURRENT LOYALTY EFFORTS

Rate your organization's current Emotion Marketing efforts according to the scale below.

*Does not describe
our organization
at all*

*Describes our
organization
perfectly*

1   2   3   4   5

1. We know how much it costs to acquire and keep a
    customer. _____

2. We understand the difference between customer
    satisfaction and customer loyalty. _____

3. We recognize the link among value, customer
    loyalty, and profits. _____

4. Our organization's leadership is committed to
    developing long-term customer relationships. _____

5. Our organization truly cares about our customers and employees. _____

6. Our customers and employees perceive that we care. _____

7. Our organization is proactive in cultivating relationships with our best customers. _____

8. Every effort is made to ensure that we deliver only communications that customers identify as being of high value to them. _____

9. We understand the total cost to our organization when a customer defects and have programs in place to reduce defection. _____

10. Our organization's desired brand identity strongly matches our customers' actual perception of our brand image. _____

11. Our customers trust that we will consistently deliver against our brand promise. _____

12. Our organization has implemented a communications program that both recognizes and rewards customers for their loyalty over time. _____

13. Our front-line employees have been adequately empowered to serve the customers at their discretion. _____

14. Merchandising and presentation of our products focuses on benefits, applications, and solutions, as opposed to product attributes or features. _____

15. Our products and services contribute to a unique user experience. _____

16. The process of shopping for, purchasing, and using our products and services helps simplify our customers' lives. _____

17. We deliver emotional value to our customers through Equity, Experience, and Energy. _____

Total _____

Rating (total divided by 17) = _____

Emotion Marketing at work

Score: 1.0–1.8

Based on these scores, it seems this business is unfamiliar with Emotion Marketing or lacks ongoing support for initiatives—even experimenting with a few relationship-building policies could have an impact on the bottom line. In the short term, tracking customer loyalty, thanking long-time customers, and empowering employees to meet customer needs can be effective; upper management should take the lead in developing a comprehensive, long-term loyalty program.

Score: 1.9–4.1

Emotion Marketing already seems to be part of day-to-day business for this organization. But there are weak spots—perhaps in customer communication, follow-through on good intentions, or management support. Developing an action plan, with clearly defined tactics for Assessment, Strategy, Implementation, and Evaluation, can help make building customer relationships a corporate priority.

Score: 4.2–5.0

This company clearly understands and utilizes an Emotion Marketing program—its leaders and front-line employees understand the importance of building strong relationships. There may be room for improvement in the details: creating personalized communications for individual customers, encouraging employees to take more responsibility for customer relationships, developing systems for tracking customer behavior, or turning "best practices" into company policies.

©Hallmark Loyalty Marketing Group

STEP 2: ASSESSING THE VALUE PROPOSITION

Answer the following questions from the perspective of an average customer and/or based on customer research.

1. List the key competitors your customers also consider when choosing your products/services:

   _____   _____

   _____   _____

   _____   _____

2. Answer the following questions using the *Value Star*[SM] model below:

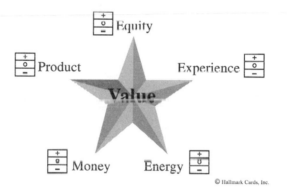

© Hallmark Cards, Inc.

⊗ *Step 1:* Based on your customer research, how would your customers rank the five value drivers which follow? *Place the number 1 through 5 next to the appropriate value driver.*

⊗ *Step 2:* In light of your current competition, how would your customers rate your organization against their other choices on each of the five value drivers as shown below? *Place a + (plus) by each value driver in which your customers perceive your organization has a distinct competitive advantage, an N (neutral) by each driver your company has neither an advantage nor disadvantage, and a – (minus) by each driver considered a disadvantage versus the competition.*

Value Driver	Description	(Step 1) Importance Ranking (1–5)	(Step 2) Competitive Difference (+,N,–)
Product	*Quality* and utility of the product/service provided	_____	_____
Equity	Overall *trust* in your brand promise	_____	_____
Experience	Atmosphere, services and customer *relationships*	_____	_____
Energy	*Convenience* in terms of time and effort	_____	_____
Money	Actual *price* paid to purchase and use the product	_____	_____

3. From the rankings above, choose the most important *plus*. That becomes your primary strength to leverage. Then choose the most important *minus*. That becomes your primary weakness to overcome.

  → Primary *strength* to leverage is _____
  → Primary *weakness* to overcome is _____

©Hallmark Loyalty Marketing Group

STEP 3: ASSESSING EQUITY

1. What is your *brand identity?* Capture the words, phrases, or associations which *your organization* would like your customers to use in describing what your brand means to them, and organize them into rational and emotional components:

Rational Components (thoughts)   *Emotional Components (feelings)*

_____   _____

_____   _____

_____   _____

_____   _____

2. What unique *brand promise* does your desired brand identity make to customers? Write a short sentence describing the primary benefit (or value proposition) your brand delivers to your customers unique to the competition:

_____

_____

3. Which basic human need(s) are fulfilled by your brand promise? (Refer to the Motivational Hierarchy in Chapter 2):

_____   _____   _____

4. What higher-level need(s) might your brand promise fulfill to strengthen your customers' motivation to choose your brand over the competition?

_____   _____   _____

5. How might you change your brand promise statement to tap into these higher-level needs?

_____

_____

6. What is your *brand image?* Capture a list of words, phrases, or associations which *your customers* believe or have expressed are synonymous with your brand:

Rational Components (thoughts)   *Emotional Components (feelings)*

_____   _____

_____   _____

_____   _____

7. Does your desired brand identity match your actual brand image? Follow these steps in the spaces below:

    a. List the words, phrases, or associations that describe your brand identity but are not consistent with your brand image.

    b. List the words, phrases, or associations that describe your customers' perception of your brand image but are not consistent with your desired brand identity.

    c. List the matching words, phrases, or associations that are consistent between your desired brand identity and actual brand image.

A. IDENTITY ONLY   B. IMAGE ONLY   C. IDENTITY = IMAGE
(Identity Crisis)   (Image Crisis)   (Equity)

_____ _____ _____

_____ _____ _____

_____ _____ _____

_____ _____ _____

8. Brainstorm at least one strategy or tactic your organization could adopt to leverage your true brand equity and reduce the gap between your brand's identity and image. Consider how you might better deliver against your desired identity or capital on the permission afforded by your customers' perceived image (permission) of your brand:

Strategies/tactics to leverage from strength (Equity)

Strategies/tactics to overcome weakness (reduce gap between image and identity)

©*Hallmark Loyalty Marketing Group*

STEP 4: ASSESSING EXPERIENCE

1. To what extent can your customers *customize* your products/services based on their own unique wants and needs?

___Individually customized   ___Some customization   ___One size fits all

2. To what extent do your products and services offer turnkey *solutions* organized around consumer benefits, rather than offering partial solutions organized around product attributes and features?

___Offer complete solutions   ___Provide partial solutions   ___Oriented around features

3. How might you provide more *customization* or *turnkey solutions* to your customers to improve their perception of value from your organization?

_____

_____

4. List some specific ways you might make the process of shopping, purchasing, and using your products and services more *interesting* or *entertaining* for your customers (for example, could you take them on a journey or tell a story?):

_____

_____

5. How passionate, committed, and competent are your *front-line employees?* Circle the ideas listed below that might provide an opportunity to improve the skills, satisfaction, and loyalty of your valuable sales and customer service personnel:

Hiring/Screening	*Training/Empowering*	*Recognition/Rewards*
Screen for affinity to your products	Provide initial and ongoing training	Implement a balanced scorecard measuring success from financial,

		customer, employee, and innovation perspectives
Seek referrals from good employees	Assign a mentor to each employee	Make at least 25% of pay contingent upon results based on performance objectives
Offer full-time, permanent positions	Provide more tools to service a broad range of customer needs	Create regular, on-going employee recognition and rewards based on individual and group contributions
Recruit from your consumer base	Empower employees to please customers at their discretion	Provide special awards/privileges for top performers
Screen for results-orientation, listening/ empathy skills and leadership potential	Encourage peer feedback	Celebrate employees' personal and professional milestones

6. List and describe your primary *customer segments* in order of importance to your organization:

Customer Segment	*Description (defining characteristics such as demographic, psychographic, behavioral)*
_____	_____
_____	_____
_____	_____
_____	_____

7. Pick one of your segments (perhaps your very best customers) and chart the *current points of interaction* (touchpoints) these customers are likely to experience at each customer stage. (Refer to Chapter 7 for *Customer Life Stages* and *Emotional EKG*.)

Acquisition   *Assimilation*   *Cultivation*   *Reactivation*

_____   _____   _____   _____

_____   _____   _____   _____

_____   _____   _____   _____

_____   _____   _____   _____

_____   _____   _____   _____

_____   _____   _____   _____

Identify new touchpoints to help meet your customers' emotional needs at each stage, and move them along the loyalty curve:

Acquisition   *Assimilation*   *Cultivation*   *Reactivation*

_____   _____   _____   _____

_____   _____   _____   _____

_____   _____   _____   _____

_____   _____   _____   _____

_____   _____   _____   _____

8. How might these touchpoints be more effectively integrated?

_____

_____

_____

9. Which key answers in this assessment will you use to deliver more emotional value to the relationship experience with customers?

_____

_____

_____

©Hallmark Loyalty Marketing Group

STEP 5: ASSESSING ENERGY

1. What would your customers say are the primary *barriers or frustrations* that make the process of shopping for, purchasing, and using your products and services inconvenient or time consuming? What are some ways you can *simplify your customers' lives* by making this process easier or more convenient?

   Barriers or Frustrations   *Ways to Simplify*

   _____   _____

   _____   _____

   _____   _____

   _____   _____

2. How could you utilize the speed, flexibility, and interactivity of the Internet to reduce the actual or perceived energy required by your customers?

   _____

   _____

   _____

3. What are the situations or problems that arise which propel your customers to recognize the need for your products and services? How could you add more value to offer a more complete, turnkey solution?

   Situations/Problems   *Turnkey Solutions*

   _____   _____

   _____   _____

   _____   _____

   _____   _____

4. How might your organization anticipate or identify these situations or problems in real time to help reduce the gap between need identification and fulfillment?

_____

_____

_____

5. What is the single most significant action you can take within your organization to reduce the perceived energy required by customers to shop for, purchase, and use your products and services?

_____

_____

_____

©Hallmark Loyalty Marketing Group

STEP 6: ASSESSMENT SUMMARY

Review your answers to the preceding value assessments. List the most important actions you will take as a result to improve the emotional value provided to your customers:

1. **Equity**—Building Trust in Your Brand

———————————————————————

———————————————————————

———————————————————————

2. **Experience**—Building Customer Relationships

———————————————————————

———————————————————————

———————————————————————

3. **Energy**—Making It Fast and Easy

———————————————————————

———————————————————————

———————————————————————

©Hallmark Loyalty Marketing Group

*Join the growing community
of Emotion Marketers at*
www.emotion-marketing.com

Notes

Chapter 1

1 Ford Motor Co. information from Associated Press article, reported in *The Courier-Journal,* October 28, 1999

2 *The Loyalty Effect,* Frederick F. Reichheld (Harvard Business School Press, Boston, 1996)

3 *The Service Profit Chain,* James L. Heskett, W. Earl Sasser, Jr, Leonard A. Schlesinger (The Free Press, New York, 1997)

4 Hunter Business Group, LLC, Milwaukee, Wisconsin

5 *National Study of Customer Loyalty* (Harte-Hanks Analytics, Rivers Edge, New Jersey, 1998)

6 "The Best Corporate Reputations in America," Ronald Alsop, *The Wall Street Journal,* September 23, 1999; research conducted by Harris Interactive Inc. and the Reputation Institute, New York

7 "Attention fliers: Canceled flights now status quo," Chris Woodyard, *USA Today,* December 7, 1999

8 "Briefs," *The Wall Street Journal,* January 27, 2000; survey by KPMG, New York

9 Survey by the Conference Board as reported in Associated Press article, *The Courier-Journal,* July 27, 1999

10 *Management Review* magazine, May 1999

11 *Blur,* Stan Davis, Christopher Meyer (Warner Books, New York, 1998)

12 Equitrend—surveys by Total Research Corporation, Princeton, New Jersey

Chapter 2

13 *What Customers Like About You: Adding Emotional Value for Service Excellence and Competitive Advantage,* D. Freemantle (Nicholas Brealey Publishing, London, 1998)

14 "Brand-building different from gaining trial," Don E. Schultz, *Marketing News,* January 3, 2000

15 "Brand Zealots," Horacio D. Rozanski, Allen G. Baum, and Bradley T. Wolfsen, *Strategy & Business,* Fourth Quarter 1999

16 The Ritz-Carlton: About Us: The Ritz-Carlton Mystique: Our Gold Standards. *http://www.ritz-carlton.com/html_corp/about_us/mystique_goldstandards.asp,* June 2000

17 *"What's Next?" Sales & Marketing Management,* Joe Marengi as told to Michele Marchetti, January 2000 (35)

18 "Under the Radar," column by Bill Richards, *The Wall Street Journal,* January 6, 2000 (B8)

19 *The Courier-Journal,* January 24, 2000

20 *Marketing Straight to the Heart,* B. Fieg (AMACOM, New York, 1997)

21 *Marketing to the Mind: Right Brain Strategies for Advertising and Marketing,* R. C. Maddock & F. L. Fulton (Quorum Books, Westport, Connecticut, 1996)

22 The Disney Institute. *http://disney.go.com/disneyworld/disneyinstitute/index.html,* June 2000

23 *Quantum Physics and Brain Science for Marketers,* D. B. Wolfe, available FTP: Hostname: iglobal.com Directory: DRM/File: a-002.htm, September 15, 1998

24 *Why Consumers Say One Thing, Do Another,* D. B. Wolfe, available FTP: Hostname: iglobal.com Directory: DRM/File: a-002.htm, September 15, 1998

25 *Emotional Intelligence,* Daniel Goleman (Bantam Books, New York, 1995)

26 "The Engines of Life," Carol Hymowitz, *The Wall Street Journal,* January 1, 2000 (R54)

27 "The Dream Society," Rolf Jensen (McGraw-Hill, New York, 1999).

Chapter 3

28 Research conducted by Harris Interactive Inc. and the Reputation Institute, New York, "The Best Corporate Reputations in America," *The Wall Street Journal,* September 23, 1999

Chapter 4

29 *Experiential Marketing,* Bernd H. Schmitt (The Free Press, New York, 1999)

30 "Welcome to the Business Economy," B. Joseph Pine II and James H. Gilmore, *Harvard Business Review,* July–August 1998

31 *The Saturn Difference—Creating Customer Loyalty in Your Company,* Vicki Lenz (John Wiley and Sons, Inc., New York, 1999)

Chapter 6

32 "Management Guru Tom Peters on Design," *@issue: The Journal of Business & Design,* Volume 6, No. 1

Chapter 7

33 *Enterprise One to One,* Don Pepper and Martha Rogers, Ph.D (Currency by Doubleday, New York, 1997)

34 *National Study of Customer Loyalty* (Harte-Hanks Analytics, Rivers Edge, New Jersey, 1998)

35 Ibid

Chapter 8

36 InterActive Solutions, December, 1997

37 "Americans Like Direct Mail," *Direct,* April 1999

Chapter 9

38 "Going Strong: The Father of Direct Marketing Sees the Future in Cyberspace," *Advertising Age,* April 17, 2000

39 *Computer Industry Almanac,* December 1999

40 Forrester Research, as quoted in "Online Buying Sprees to Skyrocket" (Stagnito Publishing, May, 2000)

41 "E-Loyalty: Your Secret Weapon on the Web," Frederick F. Reichheld and Phil Schefter, *Harvard Business Review,* July–August 2000

42 Ibid, 106

43 Ibid

44 "CRM in the Internet Era," Michael Dell, *PC Magazine* from ZDWire, June 27, 2000

45 "I'm Tired," Aaron Goldberg, *MC Technology Marketing Intelligence,* May 2000

46 "Bringing Love to the Internet," Suein L. Hwang, *The Wall Street Journal,* May 18, 2000

47 "The Dos and Don'ts of Consumer E-Commerce," Roger O. Crockett, *Business Week,* May 15, 2000

48 "On the Horizon," John Courtmanche, *1 to 1,* May 2000

49 "Bringing Love to the Internet," Suein L. Hwang, *Wall Street Journal,* May 18, 2000

Chapter 10

50 Gallup's Discoveries About Building Brand Loyalty, "It's the People, Stupid!" McEwen, Dr. Bill, *The Brand Management Column, http://www.gallup.com/poll/managing/mr000619.asp,* June 19, 2000

51 *The Service Profit Chain,* James L. Heskett, W. Earl Sasser, Jr., Leonard A. Schlesinger (The Free Press, New York, 1997)

52 *The Loyalty Effect,* Frederick F. Reichheld (Harvard Business School Press, Boston, 1996)

53 Lands' End web site, *http://www.landsend.com/spawn.cgi?sid=0963917303420&target= EDITPRIN1992&refer=NODECOMP0795&mode=GRAPHIC,* July 18, 2000

54 "The Hiring Crisis: How to Find, Keep, and Motivate Employees in the New Economy—and Steal the Best Ones from Your Competitors," Kayte Vanscoy, *Smart Business,* July 2000

55 Ibid

56 "Building Your Company's Vision," James C. Collins, Jerry I. Porras, *Harvard Business Review,* September–October 1996

57 "One Thing's for Sure—the World's a Blur," Daniel H. Pink, *Fast Company,* Issue 14, April 1988

58 Hewlett Packard web site, *http://www.hp.com,* July 18, 2000

59 The Container Store web site, *http://www.containerstore.com/pr_fortune.html,* July 18, 2000

60 "Building Your Company's Vision," James C. Collins, Jerry I. Porras, *Harvard Business Review,* September–October 1996

61 Ibid

62 "Gallup's Discoveries About Great Managers and Great Workplaces," Marcus Buckingham and Curt Coffman, *The Workplace Column, http://www.gallup.com/poll/managing/item8.asp,* May 10, 1999

63 "Gallup's Discoveries About Great Managers and Great Workplaces: People Join Companies, but Leave Managers," Marcus Buckingham and Curt Coffman, *The Workplace Column, http://www.gallup.com/poll/managing/item8.asp,* May 10, 1999

64 "Gallup's Discoveries About Great Managers and Great Workplaces: People Join Companies, but Leave Managers," Marcus Buckingham and Curt Coffman, *The Workplace Column, http://www.gallup.com/poll/managing/item5.asp,* April 19, 1999

65 Bob Nelson, Nelson Motivation, Inc.

66 Dr. Gerald Graham, Wichita State University, 1991

67 "Free Agent Nation," Daniel H. Pink, *Fast Company,* Issue 12, December 1997

68 "Strategic Rewards: Keeping Your Best Talent from Walking out the Door," Jamie Hale, *Compensation & Benefits Management,* Volume 14, Issue 3, Summer 1998

69 "Gallup's Discoveries About Great Managers and Great Workplaces: What Is a Great Workplace?" Marcus Buckingham and Curt Coffman, *The Workplace Column, http://www.gallup.com/poll/Managing/grtwrkplc.asp,* March 15, 1999

70 "Strategic Rewards: Keeping Your Best Talent from Walking out the Door," Jamie Hale, *Compensation & Benefits Management,* Volume 14, Issue 3, Summer 1998

71 Ibid

72 Poll release: "American Workers Generally Satisfied, but Indicate their Jobs Leave Much to Be Desired: Workers Are Least Satisfied with Stress and Pay Levels," Lydia Saad for Gallup, *http://www.gallup.com/poll/releases/pr990903.asp,* September 3, 1999

73 "Work & Family," column by Sue Shellenbarger, *The Wall Street Journal,* January 26, 2000 (B1)

Chapter 11

74 Ibid

Index

About the Authors

Scott Robinette is President of Hallmark Loyalty Marketing Group, a division of Hallmark Cards, Inc., dedicated to helping businesses build profitable customer relationships through relevant emotion-based communications.

Claire Brand is General Manager of Hallmark Keepsakes, one of Hallmark's largest gift businesses, with a rich history of loyal collectors. Claire has been instrumental in the development of Hallmark's consumer database and loyalty initiatives.

Vicki Lenz is a Louisville, Kentucky-based writer, consultant, speaker and president of Emphasis On Customers! Her most recent book is *The Saturn Difference*. Her web site is www.vickilenz.com.

For more information, visit
www.emotion-marketing.com